Marshall Mather

**Popular Studies of Nineteenth Century Poets**

Marshall Mather

**Popular Studies of Nineteenth Century Poets**

ISBN/EAN: 9783744674362

Printed in Europe, USA, Canada, Australia, Japan

Cover: Foto ©Thomas Meinert / pixelio.de

More available books at **www.hansebooks.com**

POPULAR STUDIES OF
NINETEENTH CENTURY
POETS.

# POPULAR STUDIES OF
# NINETEENTH CENTURY POETS.

BY

J. MARSHALL MATHER,

AUTHOR OF 'LIFE AND TEACHINGS OF JOHN RUSKIN.'

LONDON AND NEW YORK:
FREDERICK WARNE AND CO.
1892.
*[All rights reserved.]*

# PREFACE.

The following studies were prepared for a class of working men, with the sole aim of rousing their interest in, and provoking them to a study of, our nineteenth century poets.

They were reported in the provincial press at the time of their delivery, and therefrom I have endeavoured to throw them into volume form.

No material alteration has been made in either style or setting, as I am anxious they should still appeal to a wider section of the same community for whom they were originally prepared.

J. MARSHALL MATHER

# CONTENTS.

### I.
WORDSWORTH, THE NATURALIST — page 1

### II.
SHELLEY, THE IDEALIST — page 27

### III.
COLERIDGE, THE METAPHYSICIAN — page 51

### IV.
BYRON, THE PESSIMIST — page 75

### V.
HOOD, THE HUMORIST — page 99

### VI.
TENNYSON, THE MOODIST — page 125

### VII.
BROWNING, THE OPTIMIST — page 155

# I.

## *WORDSWORTH, THE NATURALIST.*

# I.

## WORDSWORTH, THE NATURALIST.

WORDSWORTH, as a poet, stood upon the threshold of the nineteenth century, and may be looked upon as its first great seer in the realm of song. Not only was he distinct from his predecessors of the eighteenth century in the fact that he formed a new school, but the direct antagonism between his school and theirs was so severe that his personality and poetry were thrown into most original and unmistakable relief. The eighteenth-century poets were slavishly classic in their style, going back to heathen legend and to ancient history for their themes. They loved the halo of antiquity: the old world was the Valhalla from which they called forth their heroes, and the fabled past the paradise out of which they invoked their deities. Gods, kings, battles, feasts—these were the subjects of their rhymes, their treatment thereof being stiff, formal, and pedantic. They shunned the common-place as subject for song. The present—that which was around them and of them—was too flat, too stale, too unprofitable for their muse. With them scholarship asserted its supremacy over humanity—status was more than soul, and the glamour of environment incalculably greater than the disposition and the heart. Thus, the wide world of every-day life was shut out from their consideration; and the realms of poetry, hidden away in cottage life and in peasant character, received no glance from their eye, no record from their pen.

Wordsworth reversed all this. He turned from history to Nature, and from classic legend to the every-day life of man. And what was more, he turned to Nature in her humblest dress, to Nature as she shyly showed herself in field and hedgerow, in daisy and in daffodil, in wayside pool and moorland pond. Not that he was a stranger to her grander, wilder moods. Far from it. For he, as no other poet, has painted her cloud-built citadels and flaming skies.

He likewise approached man in his poverty and rags. The beggar, the leech-gatherer, the idiot girl, the worn widow—all these caught his eye, and touched his heart, and started forth the music from his lyre. His words concerning another may be truthfully applied to himself, and to his methods and themes:

> 'Love had he found in huts where poor men lie;
> His daily teachers had been woods and rills,
> The silence that is in the starry sky,
> The sleep that is among the lonely hills.'

In that verse lies the key to Wordsworth's poetry; indeed, it may be inscribed over the portals of the great school of song which he established, and in which he has ever remained the central figure. He went back neither to great names nor to great deeds, but sought the men of his own age and in his own village; nor did he desire the glories of tropic climes or the gorgeous colours of Italian skies, but delighted in the mountain and moor that reared and stretched themselves around his Westmorland home.

Wordsworth was pre-eminently fitted, both by disposition and environment, for the founding and perfecting of this great school of poetry. He was a man of simple mind and of simple habits. Crowds possessed no charm for him, nor was commerce congenial. For the greater part of his life a village was his home, a cottage his shelter, a handful of books his instructors; a sister and a wife his companions, and a few men, such as Southey, Coleridge, and De Quincey, his familiar friends. His passion was for rural sights and sounds, and it is computed that during his life he walked somewhere about 180,000 English miles. He lived in the open air. The country, in its silences and in its solitudes, was his library, his study, his heaven. He could not compose when closeted in his house, and as for inspiration, has he not said:

> 'One impulse from a vernal wood
> May teach you more of man,
> Of moral evil and of good,
> Than all the sages can'?

And again:

> 'To me the meanest flower that blows can give
> Thoughts that do often lie too deep for tears.'

What, however, was still more important was the position in which Wordsworth was kindly placed by fortune. Though never rich, he was saved from the pinching poverty that forces a man to trim his style to the demands of a reading public. Thus, he was enabled to follow his ideal, and patiently await his constituency. He permitted neither scoffs, entreaties, nor criticism to force his hand. He played his own game, and in the long run he came off winner. This would have been impossible to him had he not held a small competency at command, entirely independent of literary earnings, and had he not been a man of simplest and most inexpensive habits.

It is well, therefore, to bear in mind that fortune favoured Wordsworth in his work. Poetry such as his demands conditions other than the midnight oil and the gossip of the city club. Contemplation calls for time and quiet. It cannot keep pace with hurrying feet, nor is its 'still, small voice' distinguishable amid the clamour of tongues. Nature also is rigid in the conditions she enforces before she yields her secrets. Her votaries must wait long, and wait with humble hearts. They must listen, they must learn, they must open their minds for the inflowing of her sounds and sights. Nor can they do this until familiar with her loneliness and silence.

To how many so-called practical men would Wordsworth's life have been one of mooning and aimlessness! Tramping lanes, lying under overhanging rocks, crossing wind-swept wastes, listening to waterfalls, communing with beggars and leech-gatherers, going in rhapsodies over a field of daffodils —all these to the practical man seem so much waste, so much non-productive energy. But it is not so. Whitman says:

'I loaf, and invite my soul.'

And it is even so. We must loaf to invite the soul out of its hiding-places—out of its shy seclusions. To call forth the deeper instinct, to rouse the nobler power, to coax those spiritual forces that go out towards and communicate with the unseen, there must be some other passion besides the passion for advancement, and some other end than the end pursued by the busy and the eager of the day. But all this supposes time and retirement, and demands a staple sustenance as a set-off against the pangs of hunger and the claims and responsibilities of life. This Wordsworth had. He could go out and come in at his leisure. His board was always spread, and his purse was never empty. He could 'loaf, and invite his soul,' and his soul was responsive to the invitation. He could give his days and nights to Nature, looking hard and long, listening in all patience for her truths. In London his vision would have been blinded, and if he had been called to keep his nose to the grindstone he would never have seen the stars.

Thus Wordsworth was enabled to go direct to Nature, to look *at* her with 'a quiet eye,' and *into* her with a responsive soul. And in return Nature became vocal to him, and inspirational; her sounds were voices and her moods suggestions. She was the revelation of the Divine. He says:

> 'Divine monition Nature yields,
> That not by bread alone we live,
> Or what a hand of flesh can give.'

Or again:

> 'And I have felt
> A presence that disturbs me with the joy
> Of elevated thoughts: a sense sublime
> Of something far more deeply interfused,
> Whose dwelling is the light of setting suns,
> And the round ocean and the living air,
> And the blue sky, and in the mind of man

> A motion and a spirit, that impels
> All thinking things, all objects of all thought,
> And rolls through all things.   Therefore am I still
> A lover of the meadows and the woods,
> And mountains ; and of all that we behold
> From this green earth ; of all the mighty world
> Of eye and ear, both what they half create,
> And what perceive ; well pleased to recognise
> In nature and the language of the sense,
> The anchor of my purest thoughts, the nurse,
> The guide, the guardian of my heart, and soul
> Of all my moral being.'

In writing such as this Wordsworth implied something more than that Nature was merely an external object calling forth admiration. He went further, and realized in Nature a Presence—a Spirit—breathing through her, and manifest in all her moods. The truth was, Wordsworth 'felt' the Divine Immanence in Nature. He was not a pantheist, as some suppose ; nor was he a transcendentalist. He stood midway between the two. He was not a pantheist, for he discovered in Nature a Personality: 'I have felt a Presence,' says he. Nor was he a transcendentalist, as Browning, who not only saw God immanent in Nature, but transcending it. He looked not upon Nature as a machine, started by some unseen and distant hand ; nor did he approach Nature as a museum of curiosities brought from far and near by the evolution of ages. To him it was the presence chamber of the Unseen—the abode of the Divine Being—the mighty Being who is ever awake,

> 'And doth with His eternal motion make
> A sound like thunder—everlastingly.'

Thus Wordsworth taught us that Nature is the embodiment of the thought of God.

Wordsworth, in 'The Excursion,' lays down a threefold rule of life, which may be taken as an interpretative rule in the exposition of his poetry. He says,

> 'We live by admiration, hope, and love.'

In that line there lies a threefold education—education in nature, in humanity, and in self.

Admiration! How few really admire the world in which they find themselves! To how few is it the 'presence chamber of God'! Wordsworth says men only live as they possess the eye to see and the mind to wonder. Not sight of and wonder for the startling and the phenomenal merely, but sight of and wonder for the common features of everyday life, 'the harvest of a quiet eye.' Only thus does the mind become 'a mansion for all lovely forms, and the memory a dwelling-place for all sweet sounds and harmonies.' This admiration in Wordsworth was boundless. For example, it is found in such lines as these:

> ' My heart leaps up when I behold
>    A rainbow in the sky:
> So was it when my life began;
> So is it now I am a man;
> So be it when I shall grow old,
>    Or let me die!
> The Child is Father of the Man;
> And I could wish my days to be
> Bound each to each by natural piety.'

Again, in another poem, he speaks of the 'sympathies of them who look upon the hills with tenderness, and make dear friendship with the streams and groves.' Add to this the instinct for all that was good and ennobling in human nature, and it will be understood what Wordsworth meant by 'admiration.' Surely the need of this age is culture both of eye and heart. Our inappreciation of the beauty in the world around us, our scepticism and jealousy with regard to the excellencies of our fellow-men—how these detract from and mar the strength and sanctity of our lives! We live too little by admiration. The sated eye, the *blasé* soul, the indifferent mind—where is their enjoyment, their peace, their blessedness? But the man who in his forties can pluck the 'wee, modest, crimson-tippit flower' with the same passion and joy as when he was a child—the man who can retain the same trust in the innate goodness of human nature as when he first looked up into his father's eye and trusted his father's hand—that man grows young with years; time neither wastes him nor wearies him; he lives 'by admiration.'

Further. Wordsworth says, 'We live by hope.' In referring again to 'The Excursion,' we find two characters set off one against the other—'The Wanderer' and 'The Solitary.' 'The Wanderer' is a pedlar-philosopher, a packman or a bagman, travelling from village to village with his wares —a man with a large heart and an observant mind, cultured in the ways of men, and sympathetic towards their sorrows. 'The Solitary' lives alone among the hills—a scholar and a recluse; yet withal, sceptical, moody, hopeless. Both men have suffered sorely from loss—loss of wealth and kindred. But how widely different the effect wrought upon their respective characters thereby! 'The Wanderer' is loved of all, and welcomed by all; his words are helpful, and his cheering presence an inspiration. 'The Solitary' shuns, and in his turn is shunned by, his fellows. And wherein lies the difference? In this: 'The Wanderer' is hopeful; 'The Solitary' hopeless. The one sees a future, and lives for it; the other dwells upon a desolate past, and would fain die. How well may Longfellow's words be quoted here!—

> 'Not sorrow
> Is our destined end or way;
> But to act that each to-morrow
> Find us further than to-day.'

We are cursed to-day with the spirit of a brooding pessimism. Hope is looked upon as a phantom to be chased only by the insane. One teacher has gone so far as to say that if God made this world He made it with His left hand, and the sooner He destroys it with His right hand the better. To cherish such a spirit as this is death —death in its gloomiest and deadliest form. To ward it off, and to inspire us with the thrill and possibility of life, Wordsworth raises his voice and makes 'The Wanderer' say:

> 'The food of hope
> Is meditated action; robbed of this
> Her sole support, she languishes and dies.
> We perish also, for we live by hope
> And by desire; we see by the glad light,
> And breathe by the sweet air of futurity,
> And so we live—or else we have no life.'

And, further, according to Wordsworth we live by love. Love of what? Of the true and the beautiful, no matter where found, or in whom found. The love of our kind as well as of our kin, the love of universal man as well as the caste or grade to which we ourselves belong. A love of things simple and unrenowned—love of what the proud call 'common,' and what the exclusive do not admit within their sphere. Love for the love found in cots where poor men lie. Love for the colour of a wayside flower, for the instinct of a beast of burden, for the silences of heaven, and for the wastes and wilds of earth. Listen to the lines of Wordsworth, illustrative of himself as possessed by this all-consuming passion:

> 'Long have I loved what I behold,
> The night that calms, the day that cheers;
> The common growth of Mother Earth
> Suffices me—her tears, her mirth,
> Her humblest mirth and tears.'

We speak of Wordsworth as the naturalist because he was the apostle of Nature. Not history, not philosophy not art, but Nature. True, he had the antiquarian spirit, the philosophic mind, the artist touch, but all these were subordinate to Nature, and to Nature in her commonest and, to the majority of men, most uninteresting moods. Many say they cannot understand Wordsworth. And why? Because he is so childlike. There is a subtlety in true simplicity, a subtlety that only simplicity can understand. You must prepare yourselves to understand him by divesting your mind of all pride and all preconception. Our poet did not write for clever men, but for men meek and lowly; not to tax a cunning brain, but to appeal to a human heart. Take one or two examples:

> 'A rock there is whose homely front
> The passing traveller slights.'

That is, the common eye sees nothing there but a bare, blank surface, and passes heedlessly along; but the poet's eye is caught, and the poet's step is stayed, for

> 'There the glow-worms hang their lamps,
> Like stars, at various heights;
> And one coy primrose to that rock
> The vernal breeze invites.'

Thus, at nightfall, to him who can see, the bare rock becomes a firmament of fire, while during the day it is a garden, gay with primrose rathe.

Now notice the great underlying laws the poet sees in this, and note their gradation.

> 'The flowers, still faithful to the stems,
> Their fellowship renew;
> The stems are faithful to the root
> That worketh out of view.
> And to the rock the root adheres
> In every fibre true.
> Close clings to earth the living rock,
> Though threatening still to fall;
> The earth is constant to her sphere;
> And God upholds them all:
> So blooms this lonely Plant, nor dreads
> Her annual funeral.'

Thus, the life of the primrose is linked with the vastness of creation. Branch and root and rock and sphere and universe of God are but inseparable links in an unbroken chain. A tremulous stalk, efflorescent with yellow petals, is an inseparable part of the great cosmos, and as secure as the Infinite. Though least, it is none the less a sharer of His eternal majesty and might.

Wordsworth's simplicity has often been denounced as puerility, and no poem has been so much burlesqued as 'We are Seven.' True, it is found in all the early primers, and known to most of our little ones. And yet, how tender in tone, how rich in conception! Let us disabuse our minds of the idea that it is a nursery-rhyme. It is, in very truth, a meditation upon life and death, as viewed and understood from the child-standpoint, in contradistinction to the standpoint of the sage. It is, in a word, what a little one, full of life and mirth, thinks of 'the shadow feared by man'; and as a foil to the child's views we have the views of the aged philosopher, the man to whom death is dissolution and decay. The picture is artistic in the extreme. A buoyant child—a cluster of silent graves—a gloomy sage, who sees the awfulness and inevitableness of our final doom—

> 'A simple child
> That lightly draws its breath,
> And feels its life in every limb,
> What should it know of death?'

Now comes upon the scene the grave questioner:

> '"Sisters and brothers, little maid,
> How many may you be?"'

As though there were no question nor doubt, the child replies:

> '"How many? Seven in all," she said,
> And wondering looked at me.

> ' " And where are they? I pray you tell."
>   She answered, "Seven are we,
> And two of us at Conway dwell,
>   And two are gone to sea.
>
> " Two of us in the churchyard lie,
>   My sister and my brother;
> And in the churchyard cottage I
>   Dwell near them with my mother." '

Note the relationship still real to the little maid's mind through the proximity of the graves. Sister and brother lie under the mould, it is true; but the mould is only a stone's-throw from the cot where dwell the little maid and the mother. Then the philosopher tries to show the child the difference between herself and the dead sister and brother:

> ' " You run about, my little maid,
>   Your limbs they are alive;
> If two are in the churchyard laid,
>   Then ye are only five." '

But what of that? Her brother and sister, though they run not about, sleep close to where she lives, and to where she runs about:

> ' " Their graves are green, they may be seen,"
>   The little maid replied,
> " Twelve steps or more from my mother's door,
>   And they are side by side.
>
> " My stockings there I often knit,
>   My kerchief there I hem,
> And there upon the ground I sit—
>   I sit and sing to them." '

For surely if they were only a few feet beneath the ground the lullaby that soothed them when they slept at home would soothe them now that they sleep in the grave?

'" And often, after sunset, sir,
   When it is light and fair,
I take my little porringer,
   And eat my supper there."'

What was death when she could work so close to the dear ones, and when at their side she could eat her evening meal?

'" The first that died was little Jane;
   In bed she moaning lay,
Till God released her of her pain;
   And then she went away.

" So in the churchyard she was laid;
   And, when the grass was dry,
Together round the grave we played,
   My brother John and I."'

What was death when she and her brother could romp and play so near to where the dead ones lay?

'" And when the ground was white with snow,
   And I could run and slide;
My brother John was forced to go,
   And he lies by her side."'

Then the philosopher expostulates with the child, and somewhat impatiently cries:

'" But they are dead. Those two are dead.
   Their spirits are in heaven."
'Twas throwing words away, for still
The little Maid would have her will,
   And said, "Nay. We are seven."'

That simple poem is a flawless gem, and sets before us two views of death—the child view and the philosophic; and who shall say the child view is not the truer? Surely Wordsworth thought so, for has he not elsewhere said:

> 'Heaven lies about us in our infancy!
> Shades of the prison-house begin to close
>     Upon the growing Boy,
> But He beholds the light, and whence it flows
>     He sees it in his joy:
> The Youth, who daily farther from the East
>     Must travel, still is Nature's Priest,
>     And by the vision splendid
>     Is on his way attended:
> At length the Man perceives it die away
> And fade into the light of common day.'

Let us stand by the faith of our childhood. It may not be the light of logic, but it is the flame of love. It may not be the teaching of the schools, but it is the instinct of the soul. It may not be the creed of a world out of which all romance has departed, but it is a lingering echo of heaven's truth which in childhood so clearly expressed itself in our heart.

Wordsworth may be spoken of as a king amongst those who have aspired to rule through the sonnet. While it would be extravagance to match him in this realm with Shakespeare, or even with Milton in his finest productions, it must be admitted that, taking into consideration the great number of sonnets he wrote, he can lay claim to a greater share of excellence than most of his fellow-poets. It is in these sonnets his finest work is perceptible—his loftiest teaching set forth. While he claims this form of poem as his pastime, it is none the less true that beneath his touch and inspiration it becomes a prophecy. Almost all the sins of his much-loved England he set forth in the sonnet; all he feared as to her future, all he counted grand in her history, all he sought to hand down to her coming generations, are found in these poetic limitations. The sonnet addressed to the Sonnet is a master-piece, closing with the lines:

> 'In sundry moods, 'twas pastime to be bound
> Within the Sonnet's scanty plot of ground;
> Pleased if some Souls (for such there needs must be)
> Who have felt the weight of too much liberty,
> Should find brief solace there, as I have found.'

In the sonnet, too, Wordsworth apostrophises his native land, as he views her in the distance at evening from the shore of Calais:

> 'Fair Star of Evening! Splendour of the West,
> Star of my country! on the horizon's brink
> Thou hangest, stooping, as might seem, to sink
> On England's bosom:'
>
> \* \* \* \* \* \*
>
> 'There! that dusky spot
> Beneath thee, it is England; there it lies.
> Blessings on you both! one hope, one lot,
> One life, one glory!'

And whose heart has not pulsed with patriotic fervour when reading

> 'Vanguard of Liberty, ye men of Kent,
> Ye children of a soil that doth advance
> Her haughty brow against the coast of France'!

remembering the words were written in time of threatened invasion and Napoleonic boast.

Or, again, note how Wordsworth points to the internal dangers of his country through the sonnet:

> 'When I have borne in memory what has tamed
> Great Nations, how ennobling thoughts depart,
> When men change Swords for Ledgers, and desert
> The student's bower for gold, some fears unnamed
> I had, my country!—am I to be blamed?'

Or again:

> 'The world is too much with us; late and soon,
> Getting and spending, we lay waste our powers:
> Little we see in Nature that is ours;
> We have given our hearts away, a sordid boon!
> This Sea that bares her bosom to the moon;
> The winds that will be howling at all hours,
> And are up-gathered now like sleeping flowers;
> For this, for everything, we are out of tune;
> It moves us not.—Great God! I'd rather be
> A Pagan suckled in a creed outworn;
> So might I, standing on this pleasant lea,
> Have glimpses that would make me less forlorn;
> Have sight of Proteus rising from the sea:
> And hear old Triton blow his wreathèd horn.'

I am aware all this is called preaching, and no doubt it is. The poet, however, is entitled to preach—indeed, preaching is one of the gifts entrusted to him, and for which we must ever hold him responsible. He must know our weakness and our sin; as individuals, and as a nation, he must inspire us—inspire us with high ideals and lofty aims. He must deliver us from the sordid spirit and the mercantile mood—from the selfishness of mere individualism, and the unpatriotic mania begotten by a competitive age. He must stand between us and materialism, whether of faith or of practice; he must clean the windows of our souls, and open our eyes to the supersensuous world around; yes, he must preach, whether he please or not. Only one thing he must not do—he must not prose. His words must be life, and his teaching inspiration and revelation, rather than echo and repetition.

Now, I do not know of a finer study for any thoughtful man, who seeks the moral nerve-power essential for true patriotism and true manhood, than the sonnets of Wordsworth. Let him go to them as to his Bible, and read them until the spirit of every line fires and flames in his soul. At first they may be vague, their full beauty and power dawning but slowly. This need not daunt, however. Read and re-read, they will unfold truth upon truth and wonder upon wonder. The mystic spirit of their religion will insinuate itself into the conscience; and the noble life of their moral teaching build up a manhood fearless of temptation, aggressive in all noble endeavours, and true at core. I repeat, I know of no finer study for any thoughtful man. Their truths will base a nation upon impregnable rock, and their spirit awaken to the noblest life. I venture to assert, after long study, that the best Wordsworth had to give us is given to us in his sonnets; and, what is more, in them he has given us his best in his best workmanship. For delicacy of finish, for subtle shade of colour, for marvellous force of expression, they stand almost alone and unequalled from out the seventy years of his versatile poetic productiveness.

Perhaps the true Wordsworthian's purest enjoyment is to be drawn from the lyrical poems. In them are matchless touches, and conceptions unspeakably sublime. What can be finer than when he sings

> 'Of the Sun going down to his rest—
> In the broad open eye of the solitary sky'?

Or,

> 'I wandered lonely as a cloud
> That floats on high o'er vales and hills'—

Or that triplet of verses, worthy to rank with Tennyson's

> 'Break, break, break,
> On thy cold, gray stones, O sea'—

> 'She dwelt among the untrodden ways
> Beside the springs of Dove,
> A Maid whom there were none to praise
> And very few to love.
>
> A Violet by a mossy stone
> Half hidden from the eye!
> Fair as a star, when only one
> Is shining in the sky.
>
> She lived unknown, and few could know
> When Lucy ceased to be;
> But she is in her grave, and, oh!
> The difference to me!'

In his narrative poems he is more prosaic, and too often lapses into the mood that moralizes over trifles. Here he becomes the slave of his system, not seldom seeking poetry in subjects where no poetry is to be found. There is the 'common-place,' and there is the common 'common-place.' In the former, much that is beautiful and inspiring may be discovered; in the latter, however, there is nothing; and he who works its mine works it in vain. Even the transcendent genius of Wordsworth was powerless to manufacture a silk purse out of a sow's ear. The truth is, he wrote too much, because he wrote about everything he chanced to meet. He, like other great men, possessed a passion for idealizing objects that were never meant for such distinction—the result being that, while he did not succeed in glorifying the object, he did succeed somewhat in betraying the elements of weakness in his own poetic powers. These, however, were but spots in the sun of his genius. He rose to heights unattained, save by few of the poets of his own or of any age. The man who could give to the world the 'Ode on Intimations of Immortality,' 'Lines composed a Few Miles above Tintern Abbey, on Revisiting the Banks of the Wye,' 'The Ode to Duty,' and 'Laodameia,' may well be pardoned the few puerilities and prosaics that deflect somewhat from the line of his excellence.

The greatest drawback, however, to Wordsworth as a poet grew out of those very conditions which we have already seen enabled him to attain to his ideal. While the comfort and undisturbed character of his environment gave him leisure and quiet, and while the yearly income, which was never wanting, granted him freedom from the rubs and cuffs of life, they nevertheless wrought harm, inasmuch as they kept him a stranger to the fierce fight and the galling sorrow which have made many poets sing so sweetly, so touchingly, and so humanly. Wordsworth was shielded by circumstances from the pinch that has wrung sweetest music from so many hearts. His home life was happy and congenial in its relations and harmonies —he knew little of sickness and little of bereavement. He was of an equable temperament, of simple faith, and ever free from doubt. In religion he was not vexed and plagued as other men. Hence, while he could give us—and understand as he gave it us—a character such as 'The Wanderer,' he was altogether at a loss in his treatment of 'The Solitary.' How much more would Tennyson or Browning have made of him! Scepticism and doubt, however, lie outside the limits of Wordsworth's realm. He could not understand them; and when he attempted to deal with them he was at fault. If Wordsworth's life had been more storm-tossed, his poetry would not only have possessed more pathos and passion, but a realm of truth—truth deep, far-reaching, and eternal—would have come up for treatment and exposition. In this respect his friend Coleridge—the poor opium-cursed and brandy-imbibing Coleridge—was far ahead of him. None the less, the calm and joy of Wordsworth's life, together with his stainless purity and trustful soul, enable him to give us a poetry which no other conditions could have created. They fostered in him the temper and disposition that made him peculiarly 'the Child of Nature' and put him in direct and unbroken communion with

> 'The light of setting suns,
> And the round ocean, and the living air,
> And the blue sky.'

I do not wish it to be understood that Wordsworth was not in sympathy with his kind. Far from it. He was of large heart, and loved all men. But his surroundings and temper limited his appreciation of, and sympathy with, those moods so well known to, and so well expressed by, the poets who know something of the sorrows and sins of life.

Wordsworth was indeed a lover of his kind. No man can commune with Nature as he did, and not be, for the child of nature is almost sure to be the brother of man. The student of art and of philosophy is in danger of exclusiveness and selfishness, and may be tempted to look with coldness and contempt on certain classes of men; but he whom Nature teaches learns to know and to love; he is imbued and interpenetrated with the forces and passions of the Presence which Wordsworth felt was always haunting and animating the great world around. The equanimity, the repose, the purity, the silence, the vastness —all these reflect themselves and reproduce themselves in the soul that learns to look on them in their varied and varying manifestations. They reproduced themselves in Wordsworth, and were seen in his love for his kind, his evenness of temper, his child-like trust, his freedom from envy, and the restraint which he placed upon the gratification of the basilar instincts of his being. As he himself has said:

> 'For the man
> Who, in this spirit, communes with the forms
> Of nature, who with understanding heart
> Doth know and love such objects as excite
> No morbid passions, no disquietude,
> No vengeance, and no hatred, needs must feel
> The joy of that pure principle of love
> So deeply, that, unsatisfied with aught
> Less pure and exquisite, he cannot choose
> But seek for objects of a kindred love
> In fellow-natures, and a kindred joy.'

Yes, like begets like in every realm. He who communes with Nature and becomes receptive to Nature's secrets and to Nature's moods, will, in turn, reflect her disposition in his own—in a word, he will become, as Wordsworth became, Nature's child.

I have done my best to initiate you into the secret of Wordsworth. If you would put yourselves in touch with him you must put yourselves in touch with his themes. You cannot understand him in an easy-chair, with your feet on the fender and a pipe between your teeth. No; you must go out into the realm of wonder and of beauty. Climb the hills, wander across the moors, watch the changing cloud-forms and sky-colours, look into 'the meanest flower that blows,' keep an open ear to song of bird and sough of wind, and count no object, no man, common or unclean. Thus do, preserving while you do it the humble heart and the devout mind, and Wordsworth's secret will in due time be yours. He will not chant for you the triumphs of the great, but the sorrows of the humble poor. He will not recount the victory of conquering legions, but will tell you of the cottage child whose cry was 'We are seven.' The character, too, of the man affords glorious companionship. Literary records portray no nobler example for emulation—unassuming, frugal, simple, pure. What more inspiriting, what more needful in these days of patronage and popularity, than the example of one who with unflinching consistency held on to his own high ideal, refusing the baits which offered a ready-made reputation, and bearing up bravely beneath the sneers and jeers of contemporaries? Oh, it was a sight for angels and for men! But Wordsworth was conscious he was right; he had firm faith in his ideal, and he knew it would eventually be accepted: he had firm faith in the instincts of mankind, and knew that finally it would listen to his song. Like one of his fellow-poets, when the world rejected his work, he could say: 'I shall dine late; but the dining-room will be well lighted, and the guests few and select.' There was moral fibre in Wordsworth. The world could neither turn him aside from his purpose nor hurry him towards its consummation. He marched amid men as stainlessly, and with as stately tread, as he marches in his poems. He held his head high in the permissible pride of strength. What he said of Milton, we may as truly say of him:

> 'Thy soul was like a Star, and dwelt apart:
> Thou hadst a voice whose sound was like the sea:
> Pure as the naked heavens, majestic, free,
> So didst thou travel on life's common way,
> In cheerful godliness; and yet thy heart
> The lowliest duties on herself did lay.'

Simple and unassuming as his fellow-dalesmen, fearless and free as his own mountain winds, a poet by birth, a poet by choice, he lived in the eye of Nature, and at a ripe old age breathed away his soul to Nature's God.

## II.

*SHELLEY, THE IDEALIST.*

## II.

## SHELLEY, THE IDEALIST.

OF all our poets Shelley is the most imaginative. He associates, as no other of the illustrious school in which he holds so high a rank, an 'airy fairy' form and an 'airy fairy' meaning with almost all he sees and hears. While he is, within certain limits, both teacher and thinker, his chief power lies in the prodigality of the great gifts which, apart from revelation and reason, build up their own universe, and people it with their own creations. To bear this in mind is an indispensable condition for the right appreciation of his works; otherwise the reader may be vexed and perplexed with what seems the unreal and the fantastic. Taken, however, on his own lines, and measured by his own peculiar genius, Shelley stands alone for subtle sweetness of song and entrancing beauty of vision.

If among all our poets Shelley is the most imaginative, it will be well to consider for a little while the nature and functions of that great faculty. The imagination is a creative power, purely subjective, yet gathering material from hints thrown off by the objective world—that is, from the sights and sounds appealing to it from without. Not that its creations are materialized because the offspring of the seen; rather, like the child who with its doll discovers the springs of deepest devotion, and peoples its toy house with sylph-like presences, the idealist, while starting and steering his course from Mother Earth, proceeds therefrom to 'scale the empyrean.' A wayside lily fired the imagination of Jesus, and the flame thereof scorched the tawdry dresses of kings, and threw into relief the inexhaustible care of Providence. The imagination of Shelley awoke into song at the blithe note of the skylark 'in the golden lightning of the sunken sun,' and he sang

> 'Like a poet hidden
> In the light of thought,
> Singing hymns unbidden,
> Till the world is wrought
> To sympathy with hopes and fears it heeded not.'

In both these instances the creations are subjective, and yet they are suggested by the objective and the material.

Imagination is something more than fancy. Fancy lacks power of embodiment; it possesses no distinctness of feature; it is as impalpable as air. Its forms are ghostly, and ever varying; it can neither be grasped, localized, nor recalled. It is otherwise with the imagination. Despite its subjectivity, it embodies itself in abiding forms, in unfading colours, and in undying truths. On the other hand, the imagination is distinct from mere intellectual processes and logical deductions. These latter submit themselves to analyses and demonstrations; they may be measured, tested, and confirmed. Not so, however, with the products of the imagination. Real yet unreal, embodiments yet etherealizations, on the earth yet not of it, walking the strange border-line termed by the many as mystical, they yet *are*, and demonstrate themselves in unmistakable manner. They have won battles—as when, for example, ten thousand hearts were fired with the ever-memorable words, 'From the summit of yonder pyramids forty centuries behold you.' They have changed the forms of governments, and renewed the life of nations, as well as been potent weapons in the hands of subtle statesmen. They have been the germ of many religions, and the secret of their ascendancy over the millions of the earth. They are shades in the web of life rather than coloured threads; visions rather than dreams; presences rather than forms.

Now, Shelley is an idealist. He introduces us to a realm other than earth, yet in part built out of it; and he peoples it with presences which, while suggested by outward objects, convey other and higher than outward meanings. So changed is this realm, and so transformed are these presences in the alembic of his brain, and by the alchemy of his imagination, that they become freed from all laws of matter, time, and space, and by way of illustration nothing more striking can be selected than the following :

> 'Through the purple night
> I see cars drawn by rainbow-wingèd steeds
> Which trample the dim winds; in each there stands
> A wild-eyed charioteer urging their flight.
> Some look behind, as fiends pursued them there,
> And yet I see no shapes but the keen stars:
> Others, with burning eyes lean forth, and drink
> With eager lips the wind of their own speed,
> As if the thing they loved fled on before,
> And now, even now, they clasped it. Their bright locks
> Stream like a comet's flashing hair; they all
> Sweep onward.'

> 'These are the immortal hours,
> Of whom thou didst demand.   One waits for thee.'

Here is a passage aglow with imaginative fire, yet lighting itself from the material world. The mighty course is the dome of heaven. While sweeping it we behold cars, coursers, and charioteers—objects common to the earth and familiar to the eye. From these the poet's imagination warms, the coursers being rainbow-winged, suggestive of their power of flight and sweep throughout the circle of the heavens; while the 'dim winds' neither direct nor speed them, but are trampled regardlessly beneath their feet.

Further, the charioteers are of two kinds—those whose looks are backward, as though pursued by some dread and overtaking forms; and those whose looks are forward, as though in pursuit of some prize. Both speed onward, ever onward, with wild and burning eyes, their bright locks streaming like a comet's flashing hair.

Now the imagination of the poet burns with intenser glow, for these figures, created out of the heavenly spaces and earthly objects, are made to stand for profoundest truths, being nothing less than the immortal hours waiting to bear the mortal onwards, ever onwards, towards his destiny. The charioteers with backward look and wild, fear-flashing eye are those who seek escape from a dreadful past; and yet in vain, for the flight of the immortal hours is not fleet enough for an overtaking Nemesis. On the other hand, the charioteer who looks ahead, as though to overtake some prize, is Hope, whose car is

> 'An ivory shell inlaid with crimson fire,
> Which comes and goes within its sculptured rim

Of delicate strange tracery. The young Spirit
That guides it has the dove-like eyes of Hope.
How its soft smiles attract the soul! as light
Lures winged insects through the lampless air.'

Here, then, is a truth setting forth human destiny, presented in imaginative form, the imagination gathering its materials from the earthly and visible realm.

This is but one passage—a representative passage—out of hundreds to be found in the poems of Shelley. It is enough, however, to show what I mean by the use and interpretation of the imaginative faculty.

It is also necessary that those who purpose a study of Shelley's writings should bear in mind that much of his imagination embodies itself in classic form, for he not only personifies the powers of Nature, but he paganizes them. In his poetry the heathen religions find, in part, a renaissance, with this difference, however—that while their teachers believed in the presences they supposed to be existent in the powers around them, Shelley calls them forth as abstractions of a mind ever seeking, yet never finding, some all-satisfying ideal. No one can read his poems with any degree of intelligence without wondering at the strange beings—demi-gods and personified creatures—with which he fills his world; and no one can read his life without discovering that these demi-gods and personified creatures were not so much beings in whom he believed, as creations of his ever-changing feelings after someone, or some thing, in whom he would fain believe.

For example, to the West Wind he cries:

> '  Be thou, Spirit fierce,
> My spirit! Be thou me, impetuous one!
> Drive my dead thoughts over the universe,
> Like withered leaves, to quicken a new birth;
> And, by the incantation of this verse,
> Scatter, as from an unextinguished hearth
> Ashes and sparks, my words among mankind!'

Again, in the 'Hymn to Apollo':

> ' I am the eye with which the universe
> Beholds itself, and knows itself divine;
> All harmony of instrument or verse,
> All prophecy, all medicine, are mine,
> All light of art or nature :—to my song
> Victory and praise in its own right belong.'

In the 'Hymn to Intellectual Beauty' there is this still more striking passage:

> ' The awful shadow of some unseen Power
> Floats, though unseen, among us; visiting
> This various world with as inconstant wing
> As summer winds that creep from flower to flower.
>
> \* \* \* \* \* \*
>
> Let thy power, which like the truth
> Of Nature on my passive youth
> Descended, to my onward life supply
> Its calm—to one who worships thee,
> And every form containing thee,
> Whom, Spirit fair, thy spells did bind
> To fear himself, and love all human kind.'

There are among the students of Shelley those who class him with the pantheists, and no doubt much pantheistic teaching is discoverable in his works. Others there are who claim for him in his latter days a faith in the unseen and eternal, as well as in the immortality of the divine in man. Apart from any approval of, or dissent from, these questions—questions far too disputable—there can be little doubt that Shelley's beliefs, or unbeliefs, contain a dash of paganism, but it is paganism artistically rather than superstitiously enthroned. Do not suppose I count Shelley a pagan. All I contend for is that in his search after the eternal—and after this his life was one long earnest search —he passed through the pagan phase only to find its insufficiency. This accounts for his embodiment and personification of the forces around him. He wanted One to whom he could unbosom himself, One who knew his thoughts and could fulfil his ideals. Indeed, much of his poetry is a passionate cry after this, and yet, alas! nothing but a cry.

Another feature in Shelley's character, and hence a further key to the right interpretation of his poetry, is *unconventionalism*. He recognises no precedents; to him the past is neither a god to whom reverence is due, nor a tyrant to whom servility need be rendered. He is never swayed by what has been; he never maps his course by the latitude and longitude of early teachers and mind-geographers. No; he rather sails the unknown seas, explores the forbidden lands, and rushes wildly within the precincts of the esoteric shrines. Religion, politics, social observance—all these to him, despite their hoar antiquity and restrictive power, are but superstitions, party cries, and mockeries. Here he resembles Byron, without Byron's excesses. Thus, while we turn away with loathing from the latter, we are fascinated by the daring of the former. Nor was this mere bravado on Shelley's part. He hated shams with 'the hate of hates,' and his eye was as quick to discern, and his heart to despise, as his tongue was to scath them. Looking at the religion of his age, he saw its hypocrisies: priests whose lives traversed their creed, and professors who damned others for disbelieving what they believed in only by rote. Looking at the political life of his age, he saw its corruptness and cruelty: statesmen who retained power by lies and craft, and used it for their own selfish ends. Looking at the social life of his age, he saw its artificiality and insincerity: men and women, married by law, hating one another, and, while true to the bond of the altar, false, awfully false, to the bond of devotion and love. All this maddened Shelley, and prompted him to the utterance of much which stung and embittered the smug insincerity of his age. Says he:

> 'They have three words—God, Hell, and Heaven.
> A vengeful, pitiless, and almighty fiend,
> Whose mercy is a nick-name for the rage
> Of tameless tigers hungering for blood;
> Hell, a red gulf of everlasting fire,
> Where poisonous and undying worms prolong
> Eternal misery to those hapless slaves
> Whose life has been a penance for its crimes;
> And Heaven, a meed for those who dare belie
> Their human nature, quake, believe, and cringe
> Before the mockeries of earthly power.
> \* \* \* \* \* \*
> These tools the tyrant tempers to his work,
> Wields in his wrath, and, as he wills, destroys,
> Omnipotent in wickedness.'

That this is strong language none will deny; that it is blasphemous many will assert. I offer no defence for its use, but only ask that, when read, it may be read in the light of Shelley's terrible rebound from the conventionalism of his age. To him it was blasphemy to preach the Calvinistic God, 'almighty in His fiendishness'; it was tyranny to use a popular form of government as an instrument for selfish ends; it was cruelty to hedge round a home by legal purity, and yet wink at the encroachments of the lust of hate in heart of husband and of wife. Again, I say, I offer no defence for many of these utterances of Shelley, which the religious mind will be slow to forgive. I only ask those who purpose a study of his poetry to approach such poems as 'Queen Mab' and 'The Revolt of Islam,' remembering the frenzied hate of Shelley to what he believed to be the conventionalisms of his age.

Unconventionality is a necessary feature in the character of the teacher. Without it he is soon whittled down, and shorn of the personality which is his inherent strength. When he becomes formal, he becomes forceless; and no sooner is he changed into a time-server than he ceases to be a factor in the growth of the future. Each age calls for the unconventional man. In the pulpit, in the senate, in the social circle—for him there is crying need. This may be understood when we remember that nothing is so easily acquired by a people, and, when once acquired, so fatal to a people, as *acting*. When men *seem* to be rather than *are*, when the gloss and the veneer are laid on without rebuke, and blindly valued without exposure, then the things belonging to a nation's peace are almost at an end. Hence, the need of the unconventional man. In Hebrew days he was the prophet; in the Classic age of Rome he was the satirist;

in these days not infrequently he is the poet. It matters little when or how he appears—he is ever the servant of truth and the forerunner of further advance.

It is indispensable, however, that the unconventional man should be permeated with the leaven of reverence. Without this his unconventionalism runs away with his better judgment and leads him into extremes. Under the leadership of such, reformations flame into revolutions, and truth is oftentimes overthrown in the assault made upon error and falsehood. The Greatest of all innovators, and yet withal the most reverent of teachers, bade His follower desist from plucking up the tares, lest in so doing the wheat was plucked up with them; and when storming a system honeycombed with hypocrisy, He said: 'I came not to destroy, but to fulfil.' While not prepared to yield universal and unqualified allegiance to these principles, I venture to assert that he who would rightly reform abuses must show some respect for the existing leaven of truth, and remember that before the unconventional can keep the world rejuvenescent, it must be allied to reverence and discretion.

Shelley possessed the one, but lacked the other. This accounts for much of his reckless and blasphemous writing, and makes him a one-sided and extravagant teacher. For example, what can be stronger proof of oblique vision and biased mind than the following?—

> ' How bold the flight of Passion's wandering wing,
> How swift the step of Reason's firmer tread,
> How calm and sweet the victories of life,
> How terrorless the triumph of the grave—
> But for thy aid,

> Religion! but for thee, prolific fiend,
> Who peoplest earth with demons, hell with men,
> And heaven with slaves!'

No reverent man could write words such as these. That abuses did and still do exist under the shadow of religion, no one will deny; but have they not also existed in the name and under the shadow of Liberty? Were not Madame Roland's words prior to her execution, 'O Liberty! what things are done in thy name!'? And yet, despite this, we do not drag down and denounce liberty as the author and enhancer of crimes. Shelley did not. He personified her in exaggerated forms, and apostrophized her in glowing song. Ah! it was his want of reverence that led him to look with oblique vision and partial mind upon religion, and to see no escape from its priest-created excrescences save wholesale denunciations and destruction.

Another striking proof of this one-sidedness and extravagance is seen in the following lines, in which the faith and kingdom of the Hebrew people are held up to unmitigated scorn:

> 'Behold yon sterile spot,
>   Where now the wandering Arab's tent
>     Flaps in the desert-blast.
>   There once old Salem's haughty fane
> Reared high to heaven its thousand golden domes,
>     And in the blushing face of day
>       Exposed its shameful glory.
> Oh! many a widow, many an orphan, cursed
> The building of that fane; and many a father,
> Worn out with toil and slavery, implored
> The poor man's God to sweep it from the earth,
> And spare His children the detested task
> Of piling stone on stone, and poisoning

> The choicest days of life
> To soothe a dotard's vanity.
> There an inhuman and uncultured race
> Howled hideous praises to their Demon-God.

Such a description of the Hebrew race and of the Hebrew faith, to say the least, is an irreverent travesty. The very spirit of this religion was Deliverance—deliverance from the oppression of kings and of priests and of self. Its moral law was a people's law, set up for their rights and for their defence. Its prophets laid the axe to the roots of those tyrannies that sought to enslave the conscience and the mind. Its poets sung of a golden age, a day of redemption, a King who should rule in righteousness and break the oppressor with a rod of iron; and its Jehovah, despite the cant of Levites and the tricks of statesmen, was the poor man's defence. Who delighted not in the fat of rams, but in the service of the heart? Who bade His people love mercy and walk uprightly? Who hated those that 'oppressed the hireling in his wages'? The Jehovah of the Hebrews, the God of Salem, the One denominated by Shelley as 'the Demon-God.' No man possessed with reverence, no man approaching religion with a fair, unbiased mind, would so write concerning, or would so overlook, the other and redeeming side of the Hebrew faith. This faith sprang from an idea greater, and sublimer far, than any ever fledged within, and soaring from, the mighty mind of Shelley—an idea of universal deliverance through a nation, and that deliverance wrought by the life and sacrifice of its choicest son. Your unconventional man, when leavened with reverence, becomes the prophet;

lacking reverence, he seldom rises higher than the iconoclast —and such, in many respects, was Shelley.

Another interpretative key to much of Shelley's writing is his passionate devotion to freedom. Well has Stopford Brooke named him 'the prophet of liberty, equality, and fraternity.' He fronted the world's thought just as the fire of the French Revolution was dying down, and after the excesses attendant on that strange yet formative episode had led to the revulsion of many minds from the popular cause, and the withdrawal of men like Wordsworth from the political faith of their early years. The communistic ideas born in 1789 were well-nigh dead, and a selfish, slumberous conservatism was settling upon the higher and middle classes, to the entire forgetfulness of the struggling poor. It was then Shelley raised his voice, and sang of freedom, manhood, and universal rights. The result was the production of his poem entitled 'The Revolt of Islam.' Throughout the whole of this somewhat unequal work, his passionate devotion to mankind beneath the rod of custom, oppression, and religion is betrayed; while scattered throughout its many cantos is his revolutionary creed. In this creed Shelley was far in advance of his age; indeed, many of the passages to which he gave utterance might well be used by the advanced politicians and socialists of the present day.

At one time Shelley sought to rouse the soul of the English people by the composition of short popular songs; but, as Mr. Symonds shows, he lacked the directness which is the secret of the rhyme that catches the ear and rouses the imagination of the masses. Had he been less gifted, greater success would have followed this essay. He was, however, too abstract and too philosophic; he could not come down to the unintelligent as others of his school, and yet there was strange fire in words such as these:

> 'Men of England, wherefore plough
> For the lords who lay ye low?
> Wherefore weave with toil and care
> The rich robes your tyrants wear?
>
> Wherefore feed and clothe and save,
> From the cradle to the grave,
> Those ungrateful drones who would
> Drain your sweat—nay, drink your blood?
>
> Wherefore, Bees of England, forge
> Many a weapon, chain, and scourge,
> That these stingless drones may spoil
> The forced produce of your toil?
>
> The seed ye sow another reaps:
> The wealth ye find another keeps;
> The robes ye weave another wears;
> The arms ye forge another bears.
>
> Sow seed—but let no tyrant reap:
> Find wealth—let no impostor heap:
> Weave robes—let not the idle wear;
> Forge arms, in your defence to bear.
>
> With plough and spade and hoe and loom,
> Trace your grave, and build your tomb,
> And weave your winding-sheet, till fair
> England be your sepulchre.'

Finer far, however, is the following:

> 'From Freedom's form divine,
> From Nature's inmost shrine,
> Strip every impious gaud, rend Error veil by veil:
> O'er Ruin desolate,
> O'er Falsehood's fallen state,
> Sit thou sublime, unawed: be the Destroyer pale!

>  And equal laws be thine,
>  And wingèd words let sail,
>  Freighted with truth even from the throne of God :
>  That wealth, surviving fate,
>  Be thine.   All hail !'

Or again :

> ' Life may change, but it may fly not ;
> Hope may vanish, but can die not ;
> Truth be veiled, but still it burneth ;
> Love repulsed—but it returneth !
>
> Yet were Life a charnel where
> Hope lay coffin'd with Despair ;
> Yet were truth a sacred lie,
> Love were lust—if Liberty
>
> Lent not life its soul of light,
> Hope its iris of delight,
> Truth its prophet's robe to wear,
> Love its power to give and bear.'

In those words beat the passion of a lover of his kind—one whose great soul irked the restraint of form and precedent, of kingly rod and priestly curse. Yes, Shelley was the son of freedom ; he came forth from her womb, and through his too short life he never lost the dew of his youth. In earliest days he threw aside all limitation : a parent's mandate, a university's tests, a sacred covenant of his country—all these to him were mere barriers of air. He grew delirious at the very shadow of restraint ; he hated religion because it limited thought, and he hated Governments because they levied laws upon men. Freedom was an essential of his nature—freedom in every form and in every sphere. Thought, relation, action—in all these he brooked no fetters, no limitations, no impedimenta. He claimed the universe as his roaming field, and he demanded that every man should assert his rights as a god.

There is one other feature in Shelley that needs to be borne in mind when studying his writings, viz., his intense yearning after the Infinite. After the revolt of his youth, and when the wild fires had burnt down to steady flame, he turned from the chaos and contradiction of the world without to the complex heart in his own breast. Here he discovered an individual life as great in its confusion, and as great in its mystery, as the realms of matter and of man which hitherto he had so madly questioned and so wildly stormed. He found that as an individual he needed light, guidance, power—some truth supreme that could satisfy and sublimate. He turned to Nature, looked out upon her glories, gazed at her wonders, and sought to lose himself in her profundities, and yet he yearned for more. Then he sought, as we have seen, to personify her forces—to clothe them with an intelligence so that he might hold communion with them, and find in them a response to his inward desire. But here his labour was in vain; he could not find his prototype, the counterpart of his better self. Think, for a moment, of this infinite yearning on the part of this highly-sensitive soul, of the passionate cry, of the unwearied search, of the utter failure, of the cold despair, of the helpless defeat. Well has he been termed 'the pilgrim of nature,' ever wandering, and ever wandering in search of a shrine—a shrine hidden, perchance, in distant, dimmest star, or in the solitary heart of mighty forests, or in the unfathomed deeps of ocean cave, or, perchance, in some secret retreat, where beauty imaged herself in faultless form, or love took shape, and clasped the ever-yearning heart. No such shrine did he find; he died, as he lived, 'The Pilgrim of Nature.' The poem 'Alastor,' read in the light of the intense yearning of a highly-sensitive and spiritual nature, after the embodiment of its highest aspirations, is its own exposition, and a reflex of Shelley's inner life.

I cannot close without a summary of the influences resultant from Shelley's poetry. He was pre-eminently a poet, an imaginative poet, a poet among poets, and his message has been no mean factor in the shaping of the century in which he lived. Stopford Brooke asserts that when Shelley died scarcely fifty people read his poetry, and even these failed to understand it. The young men of Cambridge—Arthur Hallam, Monckton Mills, and Sunderland—were the first to respond to the subtle charm of his writings, and they printed his 'Adonais' in 1829. Four years later his star was in the ascendant. As the political life of the nation awoke, many of Shelley's sentiments lent themselves to those who proclaimed the rights and liberties of men; and ever since, with slight obscurations, he has held his own among the immortal sons of song. Indirectly, he influenced religion, politics, and philosophy. The Church was disrobed of many mockeries, the Government of many shams, and the schools of much of the coldness and barrenness wherein they had been wont to dream in what Carlyle called a God-forsaken, logic-chopping, dry-as-dust domain. Religious revivals are not always from *within;* again and again a life-reviving wound is derived from the foeman's hand, and from the camp without the walls. Political life does not always renew its strength on promises and protestations, but rejuvenates from the stimulus of the reformer and the anarchist. And thought is not merely the product of the schools, nor does it live and thrive there only; it needs the daring flight and the wild vision. Those who care to trace to their source the religious, the political, and the philosophic revivals of the last fifty years, will find much of Shelley's teaching flowing as tributary streams. And, after all, these three great forces are the main factors of life; they are the world's great Trinity—the triune god of the ages. At times this god sleeps—nay, degenerates. Then it is the quickening, rejuvenating power is needed, as well as the prophet, with crying voice that spares not. Such was Shelley's voice—sometimes wild, often blasphemous, always sincere. Spirituality, equality, transcendentalism, the three children born of the early part of the nineteenth century, may be said to be in part the nurslings of this 'child of feeling,' this prince of idealists, this immortal youth.

Two other facts remain to be stated — the first is Shelley's peerless rank as a lyrical poet; the second, the all-important fact that he was a poet's poet. Just a word or two bearing directly on these by way of finish to this sketch.

Shelley is a lyrical poet; none surpass him in the sweetness of his song. Sylphine thoughts are set to sylphine words, their music floating towards us like the murmur of a distant sea, the strains whereof, rising and falling and lingering in our ears, create yearnings after the infinite tranquillity of which they are a dim and distant echo. In reading these lyrics of Shelley, we may best express the strange sentiments they create in the language the poet puts into the lips of Asia in 'Prometheus Unbound':

> 'My soul is an enchanted boat,
>   Which, like a sleeping swan, doth float
> Upon the silver waves of thy sweet singing;
>   And thine doth like an angel sit
>   Beside a helm conducting it
> Whilst all the winds with melody are ringing.
>   It seems to float ever, for ever,
>   Upon that many-winding river,
>   Between mountains, woods, abysses,
>   A paradise of wildernesses!
> Till, like one in slumber bound,
> Borne to the ocean, I float down, around,
> Into a sea profound, of ever-spreading sound.'

Again, Shelley is a poet's poet; he has fed the fire of those who in their day have kindled and fed the poetic passion of their age. To those who care to give a little time to a comparative study of Shelley's 'Alastor' and Browning's 'Pauline,' the indebtedness of the latter poet to the former will be easily discerned; and, as is well known, in Pauline Browning apostrophizes Shelley as 'the Sun-treader.'

> 'His award,
> His whom all honour, whose renown springs up
> Like sunlight which will visit all the world,
> So that e'en they who sneered at him at first,
> Come out to it, as some dark spider crawls
> From his foul nets which some lit torch invades,
> Yet spinning still new films for his retreat.
> Thou did'st smile, poet, but can we forgive?
> Sun-treader, life and light be thine for ever!
> Thou art gone from us: years go by and spring
> Gladdens and the young earth is beautiful,

> Yet thy songs come not, other bards arise,
> But none like thee: they stand, thy majesties,
> Like mighty works which tell some spirit there
> Hath sat regardless of neglect and scorn,
> Till, its long task completed, it hath risen
> And left us, never to return, and all
> Rush in to peer and praise when all is vain.'

Tennyson was somewhat indebted in his earlier years to inspiration drawn from Shelley; while throughout 'In Memoriam' run many of the prior poet's sentiments, as, for example:

> 'He is made one with Nature; there is heard
> His voice in all her music, from the moan
> Of thunder, to the song of night's sweet bird.'

Or again:

> 'He is a portion of the loveliness
> Which once he made more lovely.'

There is a popular idea abroad that Shelley was a sort of monster in human form — a kind of second Byron, if not an exaggeration of that great and lawless man. A greater error cannot be nursed. Shelley was as pure as a sunbeam, and as chivalrous as a knight. That a blot stains his nuptial relations is true; yet his reverence for woman, and for her inalienable rights, was one of the supreme features in his character. He was no despoiler, no breaker in upon the sanctities of home, no scoffer at the honour of womanhood. To use De Quincey's words, 'He was pure from all fleshliness of appetite.' His tenderness was that of an angel, and his love the unchanging and absorbing passion of a god. As for his sincerity, it led him to utter those cries and denunciations and blasphemies which roused so much bitter feeling on the part of the religious community. It is a misfortune when a man is *too* sincere—a misfortune for himself and for the relationships he bears towards his fellow-men. He sees much which it is impolitic to see; and, seeing it, must needs expose and denounce it. And yet, against all these admirable features in Shelley, I admit there was a dark background—a background of 'insolent infidelity,' of filial lawlessness, of domestic rashness and license. I do not forget his malign attacks upon much of what the saintliest men counted sacred, nor his wild and frenzied conflicts with the eternal limits fenced round the path of man. Yet I remember hands other than Shelley's had to do with the filling in of that background. The parent who told his son he was willing to pay for as many illegitimate children as he was father to, yet threatened disinheritance if he married out of his own order; the Cambridge friend who fed his infidelity, and poisoned his receptive mind with shameful gibes from Hebrew Scriptures; the untimely age on which his genius was cast—an age of hypocrisy in the Church, of timeserving in the State, of unprofitableness in thought. I remember, too, the fearless soul, the impatient spirit, the wild imagination, the passionate, yearning youth, face to face with all these, and much more of a kind as base and maddening. I remember, also, that he died ere reaching his thirtieth year, before time granted him his redemptive term, or a mellowing mind could yield a riper fruit. Not many men would care to take the judgment of their fellows upon a life severed by 'the accursed shears' at thirty; indeed, few would care to risk it at threescore years and ten. Remembering all this, and much more, I am prepared to stand by Gilfillan's estimate of Shelley: 'On all *other* subjects the wisest of the wise, the gentlest of the gentle, the bravest of the brave; yet, when ONE topic was introduced, he became straightway insane—his eyes glared, his voice screamed, his hand vibrated frenzy.'

That freaks of frenzy such as these possess, from time to time, the men of greatest genius is only too well known; indeed, it has been argued that they are the necessary concomitant of genius. With different men they take different forms; with Shelley they took the form of almost imbecile rage at revealed religion and lawful restraint. Remember, however, this was his weakness, not his strength; his unsoundness, and not his health. How far non-accountability excuses this penalty of genius is a moot point; and therefore it must not be ours to condemn apart from consideration, nor pass judgment divorced from scientific and moral discrimination, as to the limits and possibilities of those who are not only crowned with gifts glorious, but cursed with their accompanying cranks and extravagances.

Shelley has been called 'the eternal child.' He died ere his eye grew dim, ere his hand forgot its cunning. The buoyancy of an expanding life pulses in his poetry and the passion of undying youth runs through all he wrote.

# III.

*COLERIDGE, THE METAPHYSICIAN.*

# III.

## COLERIDGE, THE METAPHYSICIAN.

As upon the surface of smooth waters ripple gives place to ripple, so in the realm of truth mind communicates itself to mind. Man in touch with his fellow-men transmits that subtle force we call thought, the invisible wavelets of which 'roll from soul to soul, and grow for ever and for ever.' Not only is it true that 'the thoughts of men are widened with the process of the suns'; but men widen one another's thoughts as they together meet and converse. As iron sharpeneth iron, so the countenance—the intellectual countenance—of a man his friend. Thus mind does not so much create mind as it stimulates and directs it. Mind is a quantity fixed at birth, each mind in its turn relegating itself to its own order or family. The lesser minds are distinct from the greater—the sparrows do not soar with the eagles. Indeed, the lesser minds are seldom influenced by the greater—seldom sit at their feet. Here, as in other realms, the law of 'like' holds good: there must be similarity before there can be recognition or reciprocity. It is the great man who becomes the disciple of the great man: it needs a Plato to become the follower and friend of a Socrates. Thus was it with Coleridge and

Wordsworth. Indeed, we claim for Coleridge even a higher rank in the realm of intelligence than we claim for Wordsworth; yet, undoubtedly, Wordsworth set him thinking, and was for many years his inspiration. First disciple, then friend, finally Coleridge became his co-worker. Intellectual labourers were they, resembling twin stars, which, while moving in the same orbit, fulfil their own course, shed their own lustre, and retain the component parts of their own respective bodies.

It was the midsummer of the year 1793 when Coleridge first came across the poems of Wordsworth. At that time he was twenty-one years of age, and Wordsworth two years his senior. The poems were entitled 'Descriptive Sketches,' and their only success seems to have been that they roused the admiration of Coleridge. But what a success this was —a success greater far than the shouts of a blatant world, or the renown born of the welcomes of an addle-headed age. I have no hesitation in saying that at this time Coleridge's was one of the first and finest minds in England. After reading these 'Descriptive Sketches,' Coleridge remarks: 'In them I see the emergence of an original poetic genius above the horizon never more evidently announced.' In that recognition of greatness we see the greatness of Coleridge himself announced, for it needs greatness to detect greatness; and more especially does this hold good with greatness in its inception. For long years after this recognition the critic and the reading community ignored everything that Wordsworth wrote; indeed, it was more than a quarter of a century later before a world paid tribute to him at whose shrine Coleridge was the first and solitary worshipper. In 1797, four years later, the poets met, and discipleship merged into friendship. At this period Coleridge writes to a friend: 'The giant Wordsworth—God love him! When I speak in the terms due to his intellect, I fear lest these terms should keep out of sight the amiableness of his manners. He has written near twelve hundred lines of blank verse, superior, I hesitate not to aver, to anything written in our language which any way resembles it.' Nor were Wordsworth's impressions of Coleridge less favourable, his sister writing: 'Coleridge is a wonderful man; his face beams with mind, soul, and spirit. Then he is so benevolent, so good-tempered and cheerful. At first I thought him plain—that is for about three minutes: he is pale, thin, has a wide mouth, thick lips, and not very good teeth; longish loose-growing, half-curling, rough black hair. His eye is large and full, and not very dark, but gray, such an eye as would receive from a heavy soul the dullest expression; but it speaks every emotion in his animated mind: it has more of "the poet's eye in fine frenzy rolling" than I ever witnessed. He has fine dark eyebrows, and over-hanging forehead.'

After their first meeting the friendship between the men ripened, and they together resolved to form two schools of poetry, viz., the Naturalistic and the Imaginative Schools. Now, it is this I want you to follow closely in order that you may see where the two men were distinct, yet one. The naturalist tells you what he sees in Nature. He paints rocks and rivers—sunshine and storm. The idealist peoples these with the supernatural, he allows his fancy to clothe and animate them. In other words, the one is a realist, the other a romanticist. If you would trace out these fine yet definite distinctions in the style and themes of the two poets, I commend to your study the little poem, 'We are Seven,' by Wordsworth, and the fragment entitled 'The Three Graves,' by Coleridge. Another striking example, differentiating Wordsworth the naturalist from Coleridge, may be seen in a comparison of the following poems on evening. Says Wordsworth :

> ' It is a beauteous evening, calm and free ;
> The holy time is quiet as a Nun
> Breathless with adoration ; the broad sun
> Is sinking down in its tranquillity ;
> The gentleness of heaven is on the sea :
> Listen ! the mighty Being is awake,
> And doth with His eternal motion make
> A sound like thunder—everlastingly.'

Now take Coleridge :

> ' 'Tis calm indeed !   So calm, that it disturbs
> And vexes meditation with its strange
> And extreme silentness.   Sea, hill, and wood,
> This populous village !   Sea, and hill, and wood,
> With all the numberless goings on of life,
> Inaudible as dreams !   The thin blue flame
> Lies on my low-burnt fire, and quivers not ;
> Only that film, which fluttered on the grate,
> Still flutters there—the sole unquiet thing.
> Methinks, its motion in this hush of nature
> Gives it dim sympathies with me who live,
> Making it a companionable form,
> Whose puny flaps and freaks the idling spirit
> By its own moods interprets, everywhere
> Echo or mirror seeking of itself,
> And makes a toy of Thought.'

Now, I think you will have noticed the difference, and yet the similarity, in these two poems. With both poets it is evening, and both are spell-bound with its silence; and yet how different the sensations such silence begets! One feels the 'mighty Being is awake,' and is hushed into meditation; the other feels the silence too strange and extreme, and his meditation is vexed. With Wordsworth the scene is peaceful as a nun at adoration, with Coleridge it is 'inaudible as dreams.' There you have the index to the two minds. Wordsworth sees in the reflection of the smooth sea the image of the Almighty; Coleridge sees in the flaps and freaks of the smut that flutters on the grate of the dying fire, and which our ancestors ever viewed with awe, the personification of the freaks of his own idling spirit that makes a toy of thought. To fall back upon the antithesis of Hall Caine, 'Wordsworth gives us a series of realistic themes; Coleridge gives us supernatural incident possessed with the reality of human interest.'

And this is the keynote to Coleridge's poetry. He was a man possessed of an imagination that soared into the realm of the supernatural. He looked into the void, and found it peopled with presences. His was the uncommon eye that beheld the unseen. He was a clairvoyant in no empirical sense — a man who saw that phase of life whose front is from the gaping crowd yet towards the seer. Hence there are certain moods, or qualities of disposition, necessary on our part before we can appreciate Coleridge. In the first place, we must have a dash of the visionary in our nature—we must be dreamers. Dreamers are of two kinds. There are those who dream between the blankets, when their eyes are closed in sleep; and there are those who dream in wakeful moments. Dreams in sleep are a mystery—no science has discovered the strange laws that govern them; but the dreams that visit us in our wakeful moments are more mysterious still. Reverie is all-eluding. You cannot define it, you cannot grasp it; all you know is that at rare moments you are visited by it, and carried away out of your corporeal surroundings into far-off airy regions, peopled with fairy forms, and leading onward towards a vast unknown. As far as I understand it, reverie is the season when the higher forces of the soul are let loose from the lower, and the divine instincts, finding themselves free from the human, to which while on earth they are in bondage, soar off into the ethereal, where one day they will find their natural sphere. Seasons such as these visit all men. It is unwise to ignore them; it is foolish to over-indulge them. They come now and again to remind us that we are not altogether of the earth earthy, and that we are, after all, allied with the impalpable and the unseen. He who becomes a slave to them sinks into the enfeebling state of a day-dreamer; he who controls them rises to the heights of the seer; while he who ignores them falls into the stupidity and grossness of the beast. Martineau has said, concerning these ethereal moods, that the herds that low amid the Alpine echoes see the outline of the everlasting hills, and the verdure of the pine-cleared slope, as well as hear the chant of the distant torrents, swelling and falling on their ear. But man sees through nature to the eternity of God. Grandeur and glory and expressiveness all appeal to him—the mingling of something secret with his spirit, as if unseen thought were flowing from the mountains and the sky to meet the answering radiations of his soul. Are these phantoms of unreality—delusions of the brain? 'It is impossible. Call it imagination, call it wonder, call it love, whatever it be that shows us the deeper significance of the world and humanity, and makes the difference between the surface-light of sagacity and the interpenetrating glow of worship, we owe to it whatever highest truth, whatever trustiest guidance, we have.' Those are the words of one of our greatest living thinkers—the words of a man who, while he reverences science, refuses to allow what he sees with the eye to disabuse him of what he feels in the soul.

Let me try and put before you an example of what this writer means, and, at the same time, show you how Coleridge may be understood and appreciated. Suppose that we stand upon a vantage-point in some valley at sundown. Mists creep up from below, and curl along the lower levels, the hills beyond taking a sombre hue of green, or, if more distant, of slaty blue and purple. Along the ridge of the farthest moorlands lies a line of gold; while beyond, on the western sky, is a panorama of cloud-forms and sun-colours stretched and sketched and burnished by the hand of God. Around is a silence unbroken, profound; above, the eternities, the vast unknown. What are the thoughts that then steal in upon our minds? Are they not far, far-off thoughts?—thoughts of realms other than earth, of treasures other than the sordid and the perishable? Ethereal thoughts —unspeakable thoughts—thoughts we cannot even recall. We see a land without geographical limit, and we people it with those whose forms are not gross with common clay. In a moment all is gone; we are once more human; we shiver with the cold, we want our supper, and turn our steps homeward. True: but we have had our transfiguration; we have caught a glimpse of the spiritual; our higher faculties have been freed for the moment; we have been upon the mount with God. It was in reverie such as this that Coleridge wrote:

> 'O! it is pleasant with a heart at ease,
>   Just after sunset, or by moonlit skies,
> To make the shifting clouds be what you please,
>   Or let the easily persuaded eyes
> Own each quaint likeness issuing from the mould
>   Of a friend's fancy; or with head bent low
> And cheek aslant see rivers flow of gold
> 'Twixt crimson banks; and then, a traveller, go
> From mount to mount through Cloudland, glorious land!'

Now, while all this may appear so much rant to the man who never looks at the clouds, except when he questions the advisability of taking his umbrella, it none the less touches an experience felt by the highest souls, and more or less, at one time or other, felt by the souls of all men.

Again, to truly appreciate Coleridge we must have a dash of the supernatural in our nature. I do not say we must necessarily believe in ghosts; but we must believe in the existence of disembodied spirits, and, to some extent, in their influence over us. It is always amusing to me to hear men make a mock at the supernatural, and then see them five minutes after their bravado turn white in the presence of death, or tremble beneath what they cannot shake off as a premonition. The most practical and hard-headed men I have ever known have told me they have had experiences for which they could not account on natural grounds. Did not Shakespeare acknowledge this when he made one of his characters say:

> 'There are more things in heaven and earth,
> Than are dreamed of in our philosophy'?

Now, however we may deny it, there is a vein of superstition in all of us, and it is well for us there is. If it were not so, what narrow and unromantic lives we should live! We are sitting alone in our hushed chamber at the stealthy advance of the dead-hour of night. The lamp is out, the fire is low, fantastic shadows play fitfully upon the walls and ceiling. Every tick of the clock sounds like the footfall of some approaching presence, and the silence carries to our inward ear a horror other and more terrible than the cries of a tortured soul. What is it that comes over us, and unmans us? Nervousness! excitement! foolish fear! Ah, wise rejoinders, yet insufficient far! How is it all men have felt this, and at this hour, until the nations have agreed in embodying the universal sensation into the proverb, 'the dead-hour of night'—the hour when the silent and the shadowy are supposed to walk abroad? Mind you, I do not say there is anything in it. It may be superstition only, or it may not. The fact is, it is there, and the inner nature of man corroborates it by fearing it, and shrinking from it. Now, Coleridge had a nature alive to all this. Midnight with him was his hour of solemn communion. The owl, and not the lark, was his favourite bird.

He loved to call up spirits from the vasty deep, from the impenetrable gloom.

For example, take the following from 'Chrystabel':

> ''Tis the middle of night by the castle clock,
> And the owls have awakened the crowing cock!
> Tu-whit!—Tu-whoo!
> And hark, again! the crowing cock,
> How drowsily it crew.
> Sir Leoline, the Baron rich,
> Hath a toothless mastiff, which
> From her kennel beneath the rock
> Maketh answer to the clock,
> Four for the quarters, and twelve for the hour;
> Ever and aye, by shine and shower,
> Sixteen short howls, not over-loud:
> Some say, she sees my lady's shroud.
>
> \* \* \* \* \* \*
>
> The lovely lady, Chrystabel,
> Whom her father loves so well,
> What makes her in the wood so late,
> A furlong from the castle gate?
> She had dreams all yester night
> Of her own betrothèd knight;
> And she in the midnight wood will pray
> For the weal of her lover that's far away.
> She stole along, she nothing spoke,
> The sighs she heaved were soft and low,
> And naught was green upon the oak,
> But moss and rarest mistletoe:
> She kneels beneath the huge oak-tree,
> And in silence prayeth she.
>
> The lady sprung up suddenly,
> The lovely lady, Chrystabel!
> It moaned as near, as near can be,
> But what it is, she cannot tell.
> On the other side it seemed to be,
> Of the huge, broad-breasted, old oak-tree.

The night is chill; the forest bare;
Is it the wind that moaneth bleak?
There is not wind enough in the air
To move away the ringlet curl
From the lovely lady's cheek—
There is not wind enough to twirl
The one red leaf, the last of its clan,
That dances as often as dance it can,
Hanging so light, and hanging so high,
On the topmost twig that looks up at the sky.
Hush, beating heart of Chrystabel!
Jesu, Maria, shield her well!
She folded her arms beneath her cloak,
And stole to the other side of the oak.
    What sees she there?

There she sees a damsel bright,
Dressed in a silken robe of white,
That shadowy in the moonlight shone:
The neck that made that white robe wan,
Her stately neck, and arms were bare:
Her blue-veined feet unsandaled were;
And wildly glittered here and there
The gems entangled in her hair.
I guess, 'twas frightful there to see
A lady so richly clad as she—
Beautiful exceedingly!

" Mary, mother, save me now!"
(Said Chrystabel). "And who art thou?"'

I think you will see how the mystic and the weird enter into the spirit and framework of that fragment. The owl, the moan of the toothless mastiff, the dead-hour of night, the hush and silence, and the presence felt, and then seen, of the ghostly form that arrests the devotions of Chrystabel, and which, in the latter part of the poem, are shown to personify evil—all these are so blended and portrayed as to produce a picture on the border-line of that shadowy realm called the supernatural.

Again, all students of Coleridge must be more or less psychologists—they must be possessed of the power that can read and analyze the inner man. Most men may be said to live two lives, viz., the outward and visible, and the inward and spiritual. It is not what we say and do that constitutes the man, but what we feel and aspire to be. 'As a man thinketh in his heart, so is he.' But the ways of the heart, who knoweth? Who can lay bare the secret purposes, and read the interior motives, or describe the surging passions? The observant eye can tell you how a man is dressed, how he spreads his table, how he entertains his friends, what he talks about and how he lives before his fellows. But how about the other side of the man's life— the soul side—that mysterious being governed by laws other than those of earth, and shaping destinies other than those fulfilled within the limits of time? Understand me, I do not refer to that morbid introspection which is the curse of the present age, and which tends to utter weariness and loathing of life. I refer rather to the knowledge of the inner principles — the permanent factors of being — the soul. Coleridge was as familiar with the avenues of the soul as Wordsworth was with the dales of his much-loved county. He could translate soul-hieroglyphics as accurately as his fellow-poet could portray the landscape and the flower. Take the following as descriptive of the twofold effects of remorse :

> ' Remorse is as the heart in which it grows :
> If that be gentle, it drops balmy dews

> Of true repentance; but if proud and gloomy,
> It is a poison-tree, that pierced to the inmost
> Weeps only tears of poison!'

Take that poetically expressed truth and let it translate the remorse of two such men as David and Saul. Both men sinned—sinned deeply; and both men felt the pangs of remorse. With David, however, there went forth the cry, 'Be merciful unto me, O Lord, and blot out all my transgressions.' With Saul there was blackness of despair and doom. And why? Coleridge, who read the inner nature of man aright, gives us the clue: 'Remorse is as the heart in which it grows.' Where there is humility and sorrow, where the heart is gentle, the eyes drop balmy dews—dews that refresh and restore. Where the heart is proud and gloomy, like a poisoned tree, the more it is pierced by remorse the more poison in the tears it weeps. Or again pass from 'Remorse' to his lines on 'Joy':

> 'O pure of heart! thou need'st not ask of me
> What this strong music in the soul may be!
> What, and wherein it doth exist,
> This light, this glory, this fair luminous mist,
> This beautiful and beauty-making power.
>   Joy, virtuous Lady! Joy that ne'er was given,
> Save to the pure, and in their purest hour,
> Life, and Life's effluence—cloud at once and shower,
> Joy, Lady! is the spirit and the power
> Which wedding Nature to us gives in dower,
>     A new Earth and a new Heaven,
> Undreamt of by the sensual and the proud—
> Joy is the sweet voice, Joy the luminous cloud—
>     We in ourselves rejoice!
> And thence flows all that charms or ear or sight,
>     All melodies the echoes of that voice,
> All colours a suffusion from that light.'

Thus Coleridge defines, and thus he translates, joy: 'The strong music of the soul,' 'a luminous mist,' 'a beauty-making power,' 'life's Effluence,' 'a new earth and heaven undreamt of by the sensual and the proud,' begotten of purity of heart.

Or again, to the man who denies immortality—to him who limits life to time's space, and looks upon death as the end of all:

> 'Why rejoices thy heart with hollow joy for hollow good?
> Why cowl thy face beneath the mourner's hood,
> Why waste thy sighs and thy lamenting voices,
> Image of image—ghost of ghostly elf—
> That such a thing as thou feel'st warm or cold?
> What and whence thy gain if thou withhold
> These costless shadows of thy shadowy self?
> Be sad! be glad! be neither! seek or shun!
> Thou hast no reason why! Thou canst have none;
> Thy being's being is contradiction.'

Finer words were never penned. Their refined subtlety, their interpenetrating power, their masterly dissection of the very core of man's mystic being, lift Coleridge into the first rank of psychological poets.

This brief summary of Coleridge's power and parts as a poet enables me now to take you through an analysis of his master-production, 'The Ancient Mariner.' If you bear in mind that he was a dreamer—a man given to reverie, to a belief in the supernatural, and possessed withal of a master insight into the human mind—if you bear in mind his early vagaries, his tender conscience, and his unshaken faith in the unseen—I think I can make plain what to many has hitherto been an inexplicable jumble of words, thoughts and pictures.

'The Rime of the Ancient Mariner' is the record of the history of a soul, under the figure of a voyage, given in monologue by an old sailor to a youth who was hastening to a wedding feast. In brief and graphic manner the first wayward stages are described when, with the restlessness and adventure of early days, the mariner recklessly launches forth into the unknown sea of life:

> 'The ship was cheered, the harbour cleared,
> Merrily did we drop
> Below the kirk, below the hill,
> Below the lighthouse top.'

The kirk being suggestive of the religion of his fathers; the hill, the surety and stability of home; and the lighthouse, of the old beacons and precedents of the past. The direction of the voyage is towards the south—the sunny south. And when was it not so, with Youth on the prow and Pleasure at the helm? Before long, clouds gather and storms sweep: there comes the terrible awakening that life is not all calm and sunlight, not all dreams and dawn:

> 'And now the Storm-blast came, and he
> Was tyrannous and strong:
> He struck with his o'ertaking wings,
> And chased us south along!'

Soon the vessel reached the arctic cold and congealing frost—these prefiguring the cheerlessness and despair into which life's troubles sweep the unsanctified and selfish soul.

At this important stage the Albatross appears. It wing its way through the fog, hovers over the crew, responds to their welcome, and eats their food, bringing with it the breeze that thaws and sets free the vessel from its prison-house of ice. But despite the friendliness of the bird, and the blessed omens that it brings, the ancient mariner rests not until he has shot it. I would here ask you to remember that by the Albatross Coleridge portrays the Divine Presence—the inner light—that ever seeks to companion man in his waywardness and trackless voyagings, and which, when wilfully insulted and outraged, leaves him to his perverse and lonely self.

After the destruction of the bird misfortune follows upon misfortune. The sun is hidden behind the mist, the breeze drops, a calm as of death settles upon the ocean, and a despair as of doom upon the crew, while the dead bird hangs like a curse round the neck of its destroyer—a prefigurement of the remorse that follows an outraged conscience.

Then follows an insatiable thirst:

'Water, water everywhere, and not a drop to drink,'

a coppery sky, a stagnant sea, with death-fires lit up as with witch's oils, burning green, and blue, and white.

'All in a hot and copper sky,
The bloody Sun, at noon,
Right up above the mast did stand,
No bigger than the Moon.

'Day after day, day after day,
We stuck, nor breath nor motion;
As idle as a painted ship
Upon a painted ocean.

'The very deep did rot; O Christ!
That ever this should be!
Yea, slimy things did crawl with legs
Upon the slimy sea.'

There you have the picture of a man in the toils of remorse. And what follows? Moral submergement! A sinking to the lowest deeps to which a man can sink; or what Coleridge calls 'the life-in-death,' and what Tennyson means when he speaks of a man becoming 'his own corpse-coffin.' Looking towards the distant west, the mariner discovers an approaching object. At first it seems a little speck, then a mist, until at last, as it nears, it is found to be a wreck—a hideous hull, with naught remaining but its giant ribs, which stand out like prison-bars against the setting sun. Upon this wreck cling two figures—the one 'Death,' the other 'Life-in-Death.' These figures are dicing for the soul of the mariner. Should 'death' win, he dies; should 'life-in-death' win, he lives; but his life will be one of hopelessness and ruin. Thus Coleridge sets before us two kinds of decay or dissolution. The one, that of 'ashes to ashes' and 'dust to dust,' the other, the ashes of a soul in a body that still retains its life—by far the more terrible death of the two. 'Life-in-Death,' or spiritual corruption perpetuated in bodily incorruption, is represented as a woman, with red lips, and free looks, and yellow hair, and leprous skin:

> 'The Nightmare Life-in-Death was she,
> Who thicks man's blood with cold.'

She wins, and claims her own. Hence, the mariner is doomed; he becomes a moral corpse. He lives, but his soul, his better self, is dead. And how vividly and faithfully Coleridge describes this moral corruption and soul-death:

> ' Alone, alone; all, all alone,
> Alone on a wide wide sea !
> And never a Saint took pity on
> My soul in agony.'

> ' The many men, so beautiful !
> And they all dead did lie ;
> And a thousand thousand slimy things
> Lived on ; and so did I.

> I looked upon the rotting sea,
> And drew my eyes away ;
> I looked upon the rotting deck,
> And there the dead men lay.

> ' I look'd to Heaven, and tried to pray,
> But or ever a prayer had gush't
> A wicked whisper came, and made
> My heart as dry as dust.'

In this hour of despair the mariner looks over the bulwarks, and his eye rests upon the creatures of the deep that wallow and sport under the overshadowing hull of the ship. As he does so, he begins to be fascinated with the white and shining tracks made by the water-snakes, as well as by the dancing phosphorescent fires of the deep, and the poetic instinct in the man begins to work. From an admiration of this beauty he unconsciously blesses what he sees ; and no sooner has he done this than God blesses him  The moment the instinct of beauty and of feeling— or as Wordsworth would put it, 'admiration, hope, and love '—assert themselves within him, he begins to live.

> ' A spring of love gushed from my heart,
> And I blessed them unaware,
> Sure my kind Saint took pity on me,
> And I blessed them unaware.

> 'The selfsame moment I could pray;
> And from my neck so free
> The Albatross fell off, and sank
> Like lead into the sea.'

Here Coleridge touches another of those eternal truths with which he was so familiar. Redemption is open to all men, no matter how far they have wandered nor how deep they have sunk, if they have but an eye for beauty and a heart for love, even though the beauty and the love go out toward what are sometimes deemed the meanest and 'uncanniest' of God's creatures. 'The mariner had been self-imprisoned; he had been wayward and proud; and looked at life through the fogs and mists of his own gloomy and selfish thoughts. Sun and stars shone on him, and beautiful sea creatures had sported round him; but to his imprisoned soul they were hideous and loathsome.' Suddenly the prison-house of self was shattered, and he beheld their beauty and blessed them; and when he blessed them he could pray, and prayer became the key to self-restoration.

This brings us to the closing sections of the poem, the first stage in his restoration being sleep—'sleep! balm of hurt minds,' that baptism of oblivion concerning which the mariner says:

> 'O sleep! it is a gentle thing,
> Beloved from pole to pole!
> To Mary Queen the praise be given!
> She sent the gentle sleep from Heaven,
> That slid into my soul.'

Then follow the refreshing dews and rains, with movement and elasticity of limb, while the ship is blessed with favourable winds that speed her on her homeward voyage. As the mariner nears the old haven from which he started, the land seems clothed in enhanced beauty, and the Pilot comes down to welcome him; and someone else beside the Pilot—the Hermit from his grot; for what the Pilot cannot do for him the Hermit can. As the old ship crosses the harbour bar she parts her planks, and the Pilot takes the mariner into his little boat. Thus he is saved; but it remains for the Hermit to shrive him. The Pilot stands for the orthodox forms of faith and worship—the Church into which Coleridge returned, and which he so ably defended. The Hermit, in his cool grotto, stands for the High Priest of Nature. Coleridge was a devout man, and after sailing the sunless gulfs of doubt, and stagnant seas of moral corruption, he returned to the Church of his fathers. But he was also a poet, and needed something more than a 'sky pilot' and a creed-chart; he craved for the healing touch of Nature's hand, and this he found in the 'Hermit of the Woods.'

Now, in what light are we to read this master poem? If not altogether in the light of autobiography, yet in the light of that rare instinct which enables poets to describe, apart from participation in, the triumph and tragedy of human life. No poet has lived a purer life than Tennyson; yet his 'Vision of Sin' delineates in lines of fire a youth radiant and beautiful as the morning, who, after a season of unholy and delirious delight in the Palace of Sin, emerges a gray and gap-toothed man, with a heart dry as summer dust, and with mocking words for all that is pure and good. So in the 'Ancient Mariner' Coleridge gives us the voyage of self, of doubt, of sin; and also its return to light and love and home.

But surely if Coleridge did not participate to the full in the dreariness and storm, he may, more or less, have illuminated the strange poem with some touches of his own experience, or could he have closed it by saying:

> 'O Wedding-Guest! this soul hath been
> Alone on a wide wide sea:
> So lonely 'twas, that God Himself
> Scarce seemèd there to be.
>
> 'O sweeter than the marriage feast,
> 'Tis sweeter far to me,
> To walk together to the kirk
> With a goodly company!—
>
> 'To walk together to the kirk,
> And all together pray,
> While each to his Great Father bends,
> Old men, and babes, and loving friends,
> And youths and maidens gay!
>
> 'Farewell, farewell! but this I tell
> To thee, thou Wedding-Guest,
> He prayeth well, who loveth well
> Both man and bird and beast.
>
> 'He prayeth best, who loveth best
> All things both great and small;
> For the dear God who loveth us
> He made and loveth all.'

# IV.

*BYRON, THE PESSIMIST.*

## IV.

## BYRON, THE PESSIMIST.

THERE are two orders of pessimists—the pessimist of the cloister, and the pessimist of the crowd. The former are haunted by a religious melancholy; the latter by a worldly despair. One class of pessimists are sad because they have looked at sin; the other because they have participated in sin. Both complain of the nothingness of life, with this essential difference: the pessimist of the cloister sees nothing but change and decay; the pessimist of the crowd has plucked of the forbidden fruit to find it ashes and gall. Of the first order was Elijah, the stern, lone prophet, with his hopeless wail: 'It is enough now, O Lord. Take away my life, for I am not better than my fathers were.' Of the second order was Solomon, who struck the keynote of his school when he cried, 'Vanity of vanities. All is vanity and vexation of spirit.' I despise both; for pessimism is an unhealthy temper to cultivate. It is the outcome of the moral disease known as morbidity. The saint becomes less a saint, and the sinner more a sinner, as they indulge in its spirit. God is the God of hope, and man, made in His likeness, is saved by hope, and the angel of hope ever attendeth him on his path, for

> 'There lives a voice within me, a guest angel of my heart,
> And its sweet lispings win me, till tears do often start :
> Up evermore it springeth like hidden melody,
> And evermore it singeth this song of songs to me :
> "This world is full of beauty as other worlds above ;
> And if we did our duty, it might be full of love." '

Byron was a pessimist of the crowd, and not of the cloister. He had scarcely reached the age of thirty-six before he announced :

> ' My days are in the yellow leaf,
> The flowers, the fruits, of love are gone.
> The worm, the canker and the grief
> Are mine alone.'

Byron's pessimism had its root in his lawlessness, his lust, his rebellion ; and his genius uttered this pessimism in song. But how much the fearful law of environment and heredity had to do with this we shall soon see. His father was a blackguard, and his mother was a fool. All the one transmitted to the son was unbridled appetite ; all the other transmitted to him was peevishness and super-sensitive pride. Until ten years of age he was poor and friendless ; then, unexpectedly, he became a lord in his own right. His education lacked all moral discipline ; there was not a single thread of truth in the weft that shot itself across the warp of his youthful years. He early married a cold and formal creature, a pink of propriety, shocked almost at her own shadow ; while the only child born to him was taken from him by his wife when his heart most yearned for its love. What little good he had in him was battered into fragments, nay, pulverized into dust, by Brougham, in his review of Byron's ' Hours of Idleness ' ;

while his pride was soon intoxicated with the plaudits of Europe, which, from the first, acknowledged his transcendent genius. His religious instincts were outraged by the cant of the evangelical theology of the day, and the lies told about him so destroyed his moral self-respect, that he actually repeated them in an exaggerated form that he might the more outrage pious folks who sullied their own lips to blacken and defame his already blackened and defamed character. Before he was one-and-twenty, he had made up his mind to rule, and not to serve, to be in literature what Bonaparte was in warfare, and in ten short years he carried out his aim. He entered the lists single-handed to fight against God, against law, against society. The ten commandments were his enemies, and, with the exception of the eighth—'Thou shalt not steal'—he knocked them over again and again, until at last he knocked them over once too often, and fell with them in their fall. And yet he did a mighty work. He was the apostle of a new literature raised to crush the canting creeds of the mock religion of his day, and to tear off the hollow mask of propriety that hid for the time the baseness, the greed, and the uncharitableness of the respectability of England. He was introspective, egotistic, and pessimistic; but he had an eye for nature's beauty, a soul for humanity's freedom, and his heroines, for the most part, are the purest creations of poet's brain. He was inspirational rather than reflective. He did not shut himself up and think, but he moved along the world's highway and saw—saw sights glorious in their light and purity, as well as lurid in their sin and shame. But over all there hung the gloom of despair. The only strong thing he found was his own will, and this, poor fellow! he never learned to rule—never learnt that its glory was in its submission and service. He was a rudderless vessel on a tempestuous sea, cresting the waves, yet drifting towards the rocks. He was a king without a sceptre, a genius without restraint, a mighty man without moral ballast. And yet he could sing such songs as this :

> ' On Jordan's banks the Arab's camels stray,
> On Zion's hills the False One's votaries pray,
> The Baal-adorer bows on Sinai's steep.
> Yet there—even there—O God, Thy thunders sleep.
>
> ' There—where Thy Finger scorched the tablet stone !
> There—where Thy shadow to Thy people shone !
> Thy glory shrouded in its garb of fire :
> Thyself—none living see, and not expire !'

Surely words such as these came from some hidden and far-off chamber of a soul where a shrine still stood, and where the shadow of the Almighty still fell.

Nor was he a stranger to the spiritual in nature. Listen !

> ' 'Tis midnight : on the mountains brown
> The cold, round moon shines deeply down ;
> Blue roll the waters, blue the sky
> Spreads like an ocean hung on high,
> Bespangled with those isles of light.
> So wildly, spiritually bright ;
> Who ever gazed upon them shining,
> And turned to earth without repining,
> Nor wished for wings to flee away,
> And mix with their eternal day ?'

Pessimism ! Yes, pessimism ; but very beautiful, and instinct with that divine something in men that longs for union with the Infinite.

Or, if you want the stately march to the lofty theme, what finer than this:

> 'Roll on, thou deep and dark blue ocean—roll!
> Ten thousand fleets sweep over thee in vain:
> Man marks the earth with ruin: his control
> Stops with the shore:—upon the watery plain
> The wrecks are all thy deed, nor doth remain
> A shadow of man's ravages, save his own
> When for a moment, like a drop of rain,
> He sinks into the depth with bubbling groan,
> Without a grave, unknelled, uncoffined, and unknown.
>
> 'Thou glorious mirror, where the Almighty's form
> Glasses itself in tempests: in all time,
> Calm or convulsed—in breeze, or gale, or storm,
> Icing the pole—or in the torrid clime
> Dark heaving:—boundless, endless and sublime—
> The image of eternity—the throne
> Of the Invisible! Even from out thy slime
> The monsters of the deep are made: each zone
> Obeys thee; thou goest forth, dread, fathomless, alone.

I now purpose to direct you to those poems in which the personality, genius, and philosophy of the poet are most powerfully concentrated and strikingly expressed, and for this end I shall content myself with 'Cain,' 'Manfred,' and 'Don Juan.' In 'Cain' we have portrayed a gigantic, self-centred, rebellious, and pessimistic personality—one who writhed under the restraint imposed by Nature's iron hand, and who saw in her workings nothing but food for doubt, for scorn, and for sadness. He has to toil before he can eat—such is the tax imposed by earth. He can but know in part—such is the limit of a finite mind. His years at best are few and numbered—such is the veto passed by death. Against these he rages. Why was he cursed with such an inheritance, and why should he be made the puppet of his father Adam's foolery and his mother Eve's disobedience? The poem, or drama, opens with a scene in which the family group are gathered outside the closed gates of Paradise, where Adam and Eve, Adah and Zillah, together with Abel, entreat Cain to join them in their recognition of the supreme power of the eternal God, disobedience to whom has led to their banishment. But Cain is full of resentment and rebellion. Why should he worship a God who has thus measured a father's sin upon a son's shoulders? And when again besought to pray, he says: 'I have naught to ask for and naught to thank for.'

In this rebellious state he is approached by Lucifer, in whom Cain at once discovers a fascinating and all-mastering power. When they meet the arch-fiend announces to Cain the secret thoughts of his heart, he translates the silent language of his proud and defiant soul. Soon a bond of sympathy and soul-likeness is discovered between the two; both are restless and rebellious, Cain warring with Nature, Lucifer warring with God—in fact, both warring with the same force, only under different relationships and names. Lucifer cries: 'He conquered; let Him reign. He'd have us that He may torture; let Him! He is great, but in His greatness is no happier than we in our conflict.' Sentiments such as these add fuel to the dissatisfaction burning at the core of Cain's existence. And here Byron touches one of his deepest truths. Speaking of the serpent that tempted his mother, Cain says: 'The thing had a demon.' 'Yes,' says Lucifer, 'and he woke one in those he spoke to.' And so with Lucifer and Cain. The fascination wrought by the evil of the greater was due to the response on the part of the evil in the lesser—it was deep calling unto deep, like drawing forth like. Here lies the secret of every fall. When the Prince of this world cometh, he findeth a kindred something in us.

Lucifer seeks to enlist Cain as his follower by adopting two lines of temptation—the temptation of the intellect, and the temptation of the affections. In the temptation of the intellect he plays upon Cain's ignorance and limited knowledge; and in the temptation of the affection he plays upon Cain's jealousy, and shows up the favour apparently conferred by God upon his brother Abel. Let us follow these in their subtle currents.

There are two things that fret the intellect—a knowledge of sin, and a knowledge of death. What is sin? Why does it exist? Who is responsible for its origin? Where will be its final end? Then comes the mystery of death—the desire while living to lift or rend the veil—as Cain says:

> 'Since I heard
> Of death: although I know not what it is,
> Yet it seems horrible. I have looked out
> In the vast desolate night in search of him;
> And when I saw gigantic shadows in
> The umbrage of the walls of Eden, chequered
> By the far flashing of the cherubs' swords,
> I watched for what I thought his coming; for
> With fear rose longing in my heart to know
> What 'twas which shook us all—but nothing came.'

Now Lucifer promises to initiate him into these realms of knowledge on condition that he falls down and worships him, and here comes in the following:

*Cain.* Wilt thou teach me all?
*Luc.* Ay! on one condition.
*Cain.* Name it.
*Luc.* That thou dost fall down and worship me—thy lord.
*Cain.* Thou art not the Lord my father worships?
*Luc.* No.
*Cain.* His equal?
*Luc.* No: I have nought in common with Him,
   \*   \*   \*   \*   \*   \*
   I dwell apart and I am great;
   Many there are who worship me, and more
   Who shall—be thou among the first.
*Cain.* I never as yet have bowed unto my father's God,
   Although my brother Abel oft implores
   That I would join him in his sacrifice :—
   Why should I bow to thee?
*Luc.* Hast thou ne'er bowed to Him?
*Cain.* Have I not said it?
   \*   \*   \*   \*   \*   \*
*Luc.* He who bows not to Him has bowed to me.
*Cain.* But I will bend to neither.
*Luc.* Ne'er the less, thou art my worshipper.
   Not worshipping Him makes thee mine the same.
   \*   \*   \*   \*   \*   \*
*Cain.* Let me but be taught the mystery of my being.
*Luc.* Follow where I will lead thee.

Now, Adah, Cain's wife, approaches, and with the woman-instinct, as well as a keen perception born of purity and humility of heart, she chides Cain for converse with a spirit other than those of heaven, while still the same in form. She sees at once that Cain's affection has been cooled, and she cries to Lucifer:

  'Who art thou, that steppest between heart and heart?'

Then in a conversation in which Adah feels Lucifer's strange fascinating power, and is overawed with his subtility of argument and wealth of knowledge, she cries:

> ' I have heard it said,
> The seraphs *love most*—cherubim *know most*,
> And this should be a cherub—since he loves *not*.
> \* \* \* \* \* \*
> Oh, Cain! choose love.'

But Cain chooses knowledge. Knowledge fits him best. Does not knowledge give power? Does it not gratify pride? Will it not make him a god?

Then follows Cain's education under Lucifer, which we need not follow, only to note that as he underwent it the fountains of his natural affection were dried, and a rooted hatred begotten in him towards his brother Abel. And is it not ever so? Is not the whole history of the race a commentary upon and confirmation of the pride and arrogance and cruelty following an insatiable thirst after knowledge outside the realms of finitude and revelation? Those of you who know your Browning know how that great poet exemplifies this truth. In Pauline, in Paracelsus, in Sordello; in poet, in artist, and in priest; the divorce of intellect from affection, of knowledge from love, works indifference to others, and begets the cold isolation of self. Knowledge needs limitation. Love is the illimitable, the boundless. A man may know too much, know until he is miserable, know until he is proud, know until there is no realm for faith, and hence no upward flight for the soul. But not so with love. We can never over-love. The more we love the more we live; and in a deep and spiritual sense the more we love the more we know. There is a knowledge, however, that kills love—the knowledge of the cold and imperious intellect; an intellect that seeks and serves no end but self; a knowledge that refuses alike God's lead and God's limits; a knowledge spoken of in the Bible as a light that when in us is darkness. There is a love that itself brings a sweet and searching light—a light such as that that dawns upon us when we see light in God's light, and know because we are known.

Now see how this imperious and rebellious nature, intoxicated with the knowledge of evil, and of the occult, engenders the selfishness, the pride, and the cruelty that finally vent themselves in murder.

After Cain's return from his journey with Lucifer, during which he has seen the mysteries of sin and death, the littleness of the earth in the great system of creation, and the littleness of man in relation to the earth, and all the facts which, viewed alone, belittle man—after this return of Cain's he is met by his sister-wife Adah, and solicited to join in worship and sacrifice, to which solicitation he replies in the following defiant words:

> ' I have toil'd, and till'd, and sweaten in the sun
> According to the curse:—must I do more?
> For what should I be gentle? for a war
> With all the elements ere they will yield
> The bread we eat? For what must I be grateful?
> For being dust, and grovelling in the dust,
> Till I return to dust? If I am nothing—
> For nothing shall I be a hypocrite,
> And seem well pleased with pain? For what should I
> Be contrite? For my father's sin, already
> Expiate with what we all have undergone?'

There you have rebellion. Who is God that I should worship Him? or Nature's laws that I should obey them? And there, in the spirit of Cain, you have depicted the spirit of Byron.

But this rebellion and hatred intensifies. Abel appears, and, in his turn, also entreats his brother to bow down and worship, whereupon Cain is roused to greater wrath. As Abel sees the fire in his brother's eye, and the restlessness in his mien, he entreats him to seek the favour of God and join in sacrifice with him, to which Cain replies: 'I bid thee sacrifice alone, Jehovah loves thee well.'

> *Abel.* Both well, I hope.
> *Cain.* But thee the better.

At last Cain yields to Abel's entreaty, selects the highest altar, thus betraying his pride; and complains as he puts his fruit thereon that it has cost him so much sweat and toil, thus betraying his grudging spirit. It is needless to follow the prayers of the two men. That of Abel is meek and contrite, full of sorrow for shortcoming and gratitude for favour shown; while Cain's is impious and defiant. Their prayers are answered, the one by fire, the smoke and flame of Abel's altar ascending to heaven; the other by destruction, a whirlwind overturning the altar of Cain to earth. Whereupon Cain makes a rush to overturn the standing, flaming altar of Abel, which rouses the younger brother to cry:

> 'Thou shalt not :—add not impious works to impious
> Words! Let that altar stand—'tis hallowed now
> By the immortal pleasure of Jehovah,
> In His acceptance of the victims.'

> *Cain.* *His pleasure!* What was His high pleasure in
> The fumes of scorching flesh and smoking blood?
>
> \* \* \* \* \* \*
>
> Give way. This bloody record
> Shall not stand in the sun to shame creation.
> *Abel.* Brother, give back, thou shalt not touch my altar
> With violence.
> *Cain.* Give way, or else that sacrifice may be——
> *Abel.* What meanest thou?
> *Cain.* Give way!—Thy God loves blood!
> Then look to it, ere He hath more.
> *Abel.* In His great name
> I stand between thee and the shrine which hath
> Had His acceptance.
> *Cain.* If thou lovest thyself, stand back.
>
> \* \* \* \* \* \*
>
> *Abel.* I love God far more than life.
> *Cain.* Then take thy life unto thy God.

And so saying, Cain smites him upon the temple with a brand and fells him to the ground.

'Cain' is a drama in which Byron depicts the magnificence of a soul's revolt, the awfulness of a soul's isolation and despair, and the untold desolation of a soul's defeat when powerless in the face of irrevocable law. That soul was Byron's, 'Cain' being the historic fragment in which he portrayed himself and his destiny.

'Manfred' is, in part, the complement of 'Cain.' Manfred, a man of mighty genius, carries about with him the memory of a past sin—a sin dark, loveless, and unspeakable. His one desire is to forget it—to wipe it out from the tablets of recollection, and thus attain forgetfulness. To secure this he has already given his mind to study; but in vain—knowledge does not supplant remembrance. He has also wrought noble deeds among his fellows; but these do not atone, they do not bring the 'sweet oblivious antidote.' He has risen to power and attained distinction, but even these fail to lay the ghost of the past. It is ever there—before him—within him—dark, dread, and distressing.

He next seeks the aid of the spirits of Nature—the 'couriers of the air that wait on man's bidding'—and when they ask of him his business and his quest, he tells them he would fain secure from them the secret of forgetfulness. They ask of what? of whom? and why? But when they are told that it is the forgetfulness of that which is within him—which he cannot speak, but which they full well know —they inform him they are powerless subjects. Sovereignty, earth—these they can dispense; but it is neither in their essence, nor in their skill, to grant self-oblivion. At last, after further questioning by Manfred, they suggest suicide as a means of escape; but upon Manfred asking if death be annihilation, they falter in reply, hinting that if he perchance should be immortal, the immortal do not, cannot, forget.

We next find Manfred abandoned by the spirits, and standing upon the Alpine heights alone, save for the ghostly past that haunts his heart. He looks around, and sees the fresh breaking day, the mountains beautiful, and the sun opening over all, and unto all. These, however, have no power over him; their spell upon his heart is broken, and he is as though they were not. Then, with a cry of despair:

> 'Farewell, ye opening heavens!
> Look not upon me thus reproachfully—
> You were not meant for me—Earth, take these atoms!'

he seeks to hurl himself from the mountain-heights into the gloomy depths below, but is stayed by the hand of a chamois-hunter, and led away by this deliverer to his lone hut for shelter and recovery.

We next find Manfred seeking the power of evil agency —like Saul, in ancient story, he consults a witch. To her he recounts his hidden sorrow — his undying remorse. He tells her how he has sought solace in books, in battles, and even in self-destruction; but owing to some preventive fate has been balked in all. Thereupon she offers him help on one condition, viz., that he swear obedience to her will. This he refuses, his own pride resenting such acknowledgment of weakness; upon which she disappears, Manfred being left alone, crying :

> 'I have one resource
> Still in my science. I can call the dead,
> And ask them what it is we dread to be.'

We now find him in the hall of Arimanes, surrounded by the Destinies and Nemesis. As they listen to his request, that the woman he seduced and wrecked through his false love should be called up from the shades, they cry to Arimanes :

> 'Great Arimanes! doth thy will avouch
> The wishes of this mortal?'

And upon the assent of the king the dead one appears. Manfred bids her speak, but she responds not. He cries :

> 'Speak to me!
> For I have called on thee in the still night.
> Startled the slumbering birds from the hushed boughs,

And woke the mountain wolves, and made the caves
Acquainted with thy vainly-echoed name.
\* \* \* \* \* \*
Speak to me, though it be in wrath :—but say—
I reck not what—but let me hear thee once—
This once—once more.'

To which the phantom of the wronged woman replies: 'Manfred.' That is all. No more, in spite of his continuous pleading—save this : ' To-morrow ends thy ills. Farewell.' 'Am I forgiven?' cries the distracted man. 'Farewell,' is the response. 'Shall we meet again?' No answer save 'Farewell.' 'A word of mercy. Say thou lovest me.' 'Manfred' is the only response, uttered in the dying voice of the vanishing phantom. Thus the dead tell no secrets. The awful other-world affords no help.

Then comes the scene in Manfred's castle-chamber, where the old Abbot seeks to soothe his despairing soul by the rites of the Church and the balm of Gospel hope. The good old man warns Manfred of the deadly danger threatening those who follow a study of the occult sciences and converse with spirits, to which Manfred replies :

' I shall not choose a mortal
To be my mediator. Have I sinned
Against your ordinances? Prove and punish.
*Abbot.* My son, I did not speak of punishment,
But penitence and pardon :—
\* \* \* \* \* \*
*Manfred.* Old man, there is no power in holy men,
Nor charm in prayer—nor purifying form of penitence
\* \* \* \* \* \*
Can exorcise from out the unbounded spirit
The quick sense of its own sins.

To this the abbot replies :

'There is yet hope ;'

but Manfred's answer is :

' It is too late.'

And this he argues from the fact that his noble aspirations have forsaken him ; that desire is no more ; that hope is death.

The last scene is most tragic. When the demons come for Manfred's soul, he defies them, and compels them to return, dying with his hand in that of the priest, and saying with his last breath :

'Old man ! 'tis not so difficult to die.'

In Manfred we again see Byron. Like a moth around the flame, so was he ever drawn to his great characters. He could not give the public a hero without giving himself. Byron, like Manfred, sought self-oblivion. He would fain have forgotten the deeds haunting the past. To books, to philanthropy, to necromancy, he turned in vain. The religion of the age, the ecclesiasticism of the day, he merely tolerated as a superstition, as Manfred tolerated the priest as a harmless and effete servant of a charlatan Church. And yet Byron felt that his own inherent greatness, his defiance, his genius, his will, were instinct with, and proof of, an immortality, and that he himself, of himself, and by himself, through one supreme act, could lift himself out of his hell of self, and regenerate his nature by giving himself a ransom for the liberty of his kind—the attempt at which was instanced in his last years in relation to Greece.

Permit me here to introduce the following passage from Maurice's 'Lectures on Conscience.' He asks: 'Do you know Lord Byron's "Manfred"? Have you read that wonderful play of the conscience? No one who reads it can believe it to be a mere work of imagination. There is a burning individuality experienced in every sentence. Count Manfred has come of ancient line. His castle in the Alps; the monarch of mountains continually before him. He revels in the grand forms of nature; but they have become like everything else, an oppression to him. There is on him the burden of a great crime. He has power over spirits. They are ready to do his bidding, to give him anything he asks. He asks forgetfulness. That is the one thing they cannot give. What else is of any worth to him? The form of him whom he has injured rises before him. What he has done is clearer to him than ever before. He is on the edge of a precipice. Why may he not throw himself over it? What if he did? Will the vision depart? A chamois-hunter saves him and brings him to his castle. At length the destined hour arrives. A priest visits him in his dying hours, a kindly, well-intentioned man, willing to use his knowledge and the powers of his office for the good of his fellow-creature. It is in vain. What are subordinate agents to him? He is face to face with the powers of good and evil. Which is the stronger? Which is to prevail?'

We may speak of 'Don Juan' as Byron's autobiography written by his own hands in letters of fire. There are some who denounce the production as a slough of filth. It is, however, far from this. Indeed, it is a magnificent poem, depicting the gradual fall of a magnificently rebellious soul.

A great teacher has said 'that in "Don Juan" we have the commandments written anew, by one who had broken them.' That there is ribaldry, and even bestiality, in the poem, I admit, but there is grandeur and sanctity also. He who wrote it was half angel and half devil, and the two meet in conflicting forces in this, his most colossal work. He started life with genius, with affection, with deep religious instincts; but to these were allied, through the cruel law of heredity, all that was base in a father, and all that was foolish and reckless in a mother. His surroundings also favoured the fostering in him of all that was bad. Yet, for all this, there was genius, affection, and awe. But he determined, calmly determined, that his lusts should have their freedom, and his rebellious will its own wild way. He said to evil, 'Be thou my good,' and to all law and restraint, 'Be ye far from me.' There was scarcely a doubt he did not cherish, scarcely a scorn he did not nurse, scarcely a sin he did not commit. And yet in his downward course the better nature of the man did brave battle—again and again the angel strove for mastery, and the demon was laid. But the strife was unequal, for Byron willed the bad; he threw the balance of his moral being on the darker side, and lent the impetus of his own will to the lower rather than to the higher plane. He mocked at God, he scoffed at chastity, he delighted to outrage public opinion, he hated his age, he was out of joint with his country, and he added to his own actual sins a deeper dye by exaggerating them when he recounted them, and by encouraging the gossips, who, by their lies, sought to make him ten times worse than he was. Yet all through this wild and ungovernable career the angel was avenging itself upon the devil. It avenged itself in fits of fearful remorse, in moods of low-spiritedness, in flashes of lurid flame that leaped up to scorch, with writhing worm that knew no death. It avenged itself in gradually withdrawing itself—withdrawing itself from imagination, so that nature lost its soothing power; from affection, so that the friendship of man no longer charmed or brought peace. Downward he fell, his mighty genius powerless to stay him—nay, indeed, accelerating his descent; and yet, withal, the man knowing whither he was going—counting the stages of his fall, and marking them off in this great poem—a warning rather than an incentive to those who read. If he had been a weaker man he would have saved himself; if he had been a wickeder man he would not have fallen so far. But his was the moral wreck of a Titan; it was the collapse of an archangel. The sense of sin made him sin more, and if he had sinned more deeply his sin would not have told against him as it did. And then, when the end came, Byron sat upon the ruins of his life, and sketched them in 'Don Juan.' But with what a pen! A pen corroded by drops of that hot ink we call remorse, pricking and burning its characters indelibly in canto after canto, setting forth the degeneration of the fine-spirited boy—neglected, pampered, poisoned by foolish parentage—to the last and lowest stage of a degenerate and blasé roué; his own corpse-coffin—a sepulchre of dead men's bones.

But, you say, why could not Byron have given us the history of his ruin without the ribaldry and filth that mar the poem, and make 'Don Juan' dangerous reading to the young and offensive reading to the chaste? Did you ever see a ruin without its lizards, its dank, rank grass, and stagnant pools? No; nor did you ever see a moral wreck without its attendants of evil. That Byron might have clothed it in less realistic form, I admit. That this would have added beauty to the poem I also admit. But, then, Byron hated his age. Had it not hated him? tried to crush him, and failed? Had not its canting evangelicalism, its religious hypocrisies and shams, sought to damn him, dared to misrepresent him, and actually socially ostracized him? So here was his revenge—here was the interest paid back a thousand-fold. Thus, the faiths men loved were assailed, the laws they reverenced hurled back in their faces by the arm of a giant law-breaker; the morals they respected held up to scorn, and the devil's vocabulary of bestiality, as well as his harem of lust, ransacked for all that was worst and basest in them to make mud balls—nay, hell balls—wherewith to bespatter the delicate faces and pure garments of what he believed to be a false religion and quasi-moral age. Nevertheless, I turn to 'Don Juan' again and again—not for its filth, but for its force; not for its dark pictures, but for its terrible lessons. The metre is stately and seldom halts; the philosophy is profound and all-conclusive; the wit is keen with the edge of genius, the pictures are portrayed with an artist-hand, the fund of information crammed into its verses encyclopædic, and the whole, the grandest work of a man—grand in his genius and grand in his fall. I read it with tears, and not laughter. I read it as I would read a life-tragedy, and not as I would read a shilling shocker; and I read it with the verse of Browning ringing in my ears :

> 'It's wiser being good than bad.
> It's safer being meek than fierce.
> It's fitter being sane than mad.
> My own hope is a sun will pierce
> The thickest cloud earth ever stretched.
> That, after last, returns the first,
> Though a wide compass round be fetched.
> That what began best can't end worst,
> Nor what God blessed once prove accurst.'

# V.

*HOOD, THE HUMORIST.*

## V.

## HOOD, THE HUMORIST.

IN what sense may a poet be a humorist? So far, we have associated the poet with the beautiful, the mystical, and the gloomy and grand—is it possible to further associate him with

> 'Sport, that wrinkled Care derides,
> And Laughter holding both his sides?'

Yes! I think it is. Already the poet has introduced us to the sorrows of life, and taught us to weep with those who weep; why should he not introduce us to its mirthfulness and frolic, and so teach us to rejoice with those who joy? Comedy, as well as tragedy, makes up no little of man's experience, and there is food for laughter as for tears. There are glints and gleams that fall athwart the gloom of our existence; and dull indeed is his eye who sees them not, and heavy his heart who responds not to their playfulness and light. The comic, the amusing, the grotesque—these form part of the gentle by-play the Good Father grants His children; and laughter is as much a right and rational attitude on the part of man as solemn litany or sober speech.

Now, as the poet sees deeper, and sees more truly, than his brethren, and as there is mirth as well as beauty and grandeur and sadness in life, there will be from time to time among the sons of song those who call forth for us, and present to us, this mirthful and comical element. Hood was such an one. He loved to take his readers where the vein of humour was discoverable. He loved to raise his gentle hand and playfully point to the ridiculous and to the absurd. He loved to rouse the hearty, genial laugh, and thus cheer men along the fagging, dragging road of life. He loved to sing so as to loosen the muscles of faces rigid with care and sad with disappointment. In a word, Hood was a humorist, playful, gentle, loving.

Here it is well you should distinguish between humour, satire, and sarcasm. *Sarcasm* is reckless and relentless. It is administered in a cruel spirit, and for a spiteful end. It is derived from an old word that means 'stripping the flesh from the bones,' and is in literary warfare cruel rather than critical, and unprincipled rather than just. Carlyle calls it the 'language of the devil.' *Satire*, on the other hand, is keen and severe, but never brutal. It is free from the spirit of hate, and, while wounding, leaves not behind it the festering sore nor the fatal thrust. But *humour* is a gentle thing; it administers its rebukes in mirthfulness—but, mind you, they are none the less rebukes—and it carries home conviction under the guise of pleasantry. As an example of sarcasm, take Byron's attack upon Coleridge, who had chanced to write a poem on an ass:

> 'Yet none in lofty numbers can surpass
> The bard who soars to elegize an ass.
> How well the subject suits his noble mind!
> A fellow-feeling makes us wondrous kind.'

Language such as that is coarse and brutal—uncalled for, and unwarrantable even if true.

As an example of satire take the following from Ruskin: 'If a man spends lavishly upon his library you call him mad—a bibliomaniac. But you never call a man a horse-maniac, though men ruin themselves every day by their horses, and you don't hear of people ruining themselves by their books.' There you have a keen and dexter stroke; but there is nothing brutal nor unkind about it.

And now for a sample of humour from the prince of humorists, Charles Lamb. When once asked by a lady, who had been gushing over a baby: 'How do you like babies, Mr. Lamb?' he replied: 'Boiled, madam.' And upon another occasion, when, after turning up late for several successive mornings at the India Office, he was called into the directors' room and asked the reason of his delinquencies, he said: 'Well, gentlemen, if I come late, I always go away early.'

Humour must also be distinguished from buffoonery, from ribaldry and burlesque. The genuine humorist never drops to the lower plane by seeking to tickle an unlawful appetite. He is always pure—he speaks with a clean tongue out of the fulness of a clean heart. He never walks where the angels fear to tread, nor does he reach over to the forbidden fruit. It is a thousand pities that laughter should so often be allied to the lewd, and that the only scintillations of mirth, with too many, should flash from the devil's dross-heaps rather than from the pleasant path of lawful jollity. In a word, humour is gentle, pure, and instructive, inasmuch as it is allied to the moral and the didactic. It is the by-play of noble natures making for serious ends. Thackeray has admirably defined humour as 'a combination of wit and love.' Note the union. A wag may have the former; but he only is the humorist who touches the heart as well as rouses the laugh, and who can blend smiles with tears, and so combine the minors with the fantasias as to call forth the music of the dual man.

The holiest men have not shrunk from using humour; and in showing men their folly, and in reclaiming them from their sins, it has played a useful part in all schools. Thus, there is no reason why the humorist may not be the teacher and the poet. There is a proverb that men prefer to be tickled rather than taught; it is also true they prefer to be tickled while being taught. Oftentimes the light and airy touch of a wit such as Hood is a more potent weapon in the field of truth than the lucubrations of the philosopher and the logic of the schools. We have need to thank God that we can see through smiles as well as through tears, and that laughter wings the soul as much as 'chant and solemn litany.' He who dowered man with the humorous instinct will never forbid, but bless, its rational play; and the apostle of mirth is as much the anointed of the Lord as the weeping prophet of old. It is a mistake to think that humour is opposed either to earnestness or truth. Many of the men who have been the most deadly in earnest have had merry hearts and cheerful countenances; and although Tom Hood could scarcely open his lips, or put pen to paper, without uttering or recording a pun, there were few men of his day who felt more deeply, or who taught more truly. This, however, we shall see as we proceed.

Hood's life was a very beautiful one—beautiful in its

sadness, in its sweetness, and in its resignation. Strange to say, he who made others smile, himself wept oft and sore. He brought into this world the germ of a pulmonary affection, which, developing into hæmorrhage of the lungs, carried him off to an early grave; and he was prompted to say in one of his paroxysms: 'For my epitaph write: "Here lies a man who spat more blood and made more puns than any man in England."' But afterwards his request was that his tomb might bear but one distinguishing line—'He sang the Song of the Shirt.' Throughout the whole of his life he was tortured with an overwrought nervous system, super-sensitive to noise and shock of all kinds; and through his over-trustfulness he was all his days burdened with a load of debt. Owing to this, he was never independent of publishers, who worked him as their hack, and, to use the phrase of a modern author, 'kicked his brains up and down Paternoster Row to keep their feet warm.' As a father he was gentle, considerate, and loving. He would steal upstairs when his little ones lay asleep to place his comic sketches upon their counterpanes, and in the morning stealthily peep through the half-open door and watch with delight their childish glee. He was devout and religious—not perhaps as the orthodox count religion, but as the Apostle counted it when he said, 'Pure religion and undefiled is this: to visit the widows and orphans in their afflictions, and keep one's self unspotted from the flesh.' Shortly before his death, in one of those suddenly changing moods so common to pulmonary disease, when to day seems an assurance of decease, and to morrow of recovery, he penned the following lines, the last product of his genius:

'Farewell, life! my senses swim;
And the world is growing dim;
Thronging shadows cloud the light,
Like the advent of the night—
Colder, colder, colder still,—
Upwards steals a vapour's chill—
Strong the earthly odour grows—
I smell the Mould above the Rose!

'Welcome, life! the spirit strives!
Strength returns, and hope revives;
Cloudy fears and hopes forlorn
Fly like shadows of the Morn,—
O'er the earth there comes a bloom—
Sunny light for sullen gloom,
Warm perfume for vapours cold—
I smell the Rose above the Mould!'

Oh, rare and tender-hearted Hood! As gentle as a child, as patient as a saint, as pure as an angel; in suffering as silent as a martyr; under misfortune as cheerful and radiant as a seraph; forgetting his sorrow that he might cheer his fellows, and hiding his sickness and his grief that he might buoy up wife and children. Even on his deathbed, when worn to a skeleton by much blood-spitting and waste of lung tissue, and smarting beneath the application of a mustard-plaster applied by the doctor's orders, he could smile and say to his wife: 'My dear! did you ever see so much mustard to so little meat before?'

Hood was London-bred, and of the so-called 'Cockney School.' He was a city man and a city poet. Unlike Wordsworth, he climbed no hills, nor wandered amid wastes of moorland. Unlike Byron, ancient history and the drama appealed not to his muse. But the crowd— the crowd with its sins and sorrows; its broken hearts and wasted lives; the Nemesis of wealth, the tragedy of poverty; the playfulness and innocence of the child-life; the drawn blind, the hushed room, the silent tear—of these he sang as only one could sing, who had witnessed and experienced something of them all.

He has left us a charming reminiscence of his boyhood at Clapham Academy, where he 'was birched and bred;' and among many beautiful verses, none surpass—

> ' Ay, there's the playground! there's the lime
> Beneath whose shade in summer's prime
>     So wildly I have read !—
> Who sits there *now*, and skims the cream
> Of young Romance, and weaves a dream
>     Of love and cottage-bread ?'

As we have said, Hood was a devout man, although anything but sanctimonious. Upon one occasion his religion was attacked by a narrow-minded Scotchman of the name of Rae Wilson. It seems that Hood, in one of his poems, had likened something to a sow, from whose jaw a cabbage-sprout

> ' Protruded, as the dove so stanch
> For peace supports an olive-branch.'

Whereupon Wilson at once accused him of blasphemy, contending that such burlesque had reference to the Holy Ghost. Our poet at once replied in a chaste yet witty and trenchant ode, in which we get side-lights of his own beautiful and deeply religious life. In this poem he says:

> ' I'm not a saint.
> Not one of those self-constituted saints,
> Quacks—not physicians—in the cure of souls,
> Censors who sniff out mortal taints,
> And call the devil over his own coals.'

Then, proceeding to describe himself as he knows himself:

> 'There wants a certain cast about the eye;
> A certain lifting of the nose's tip;
> A certain curling of the nether lip,
> In scorn of all that is, beneath the sky;
> In brief, it is an aspect deleterious,
> A face decidedly not serious,
> A face profane, that would not do at all
> To make a face at Exeter Hall.'

But for all this Hood claims to be religious. He says:

> 'I do enjoy this bounteous, beauteous earth;
> And dote upon a jest,
> "Within the limits of becoming mirth."
>
> \* \* \* \* \* \*
>
> I own I laugh at over-righteous men,
> I own I shake my sides at ranters,
> And treat sham Abram saints with wicked banters.
> I've no ambition to enact the spy
> On fellow-souls, a spiritual pry.
>
> \* \* \* \* \* \*
>
> For I consider faith and prayers
> Amongst the privatest of men's affairs.'

Hood then goes on to declare he has no sympathy whatever with Rae Wilson and his school in their attempt to force religious observance on the people by the enactment of laws of Parliament:

> 'No solemn sanctimonious face I pull,
> Nor think I'm pious when I'm only bilious—
> Nor study in my sanctum supercilious
> To frame a Sabbath bill or forge a Bull.
> I pray for grace—repent each sinful act—
> Peruse, but underneath the rose, my Bible:
> And love my neighbour, far too well, in fact,
> To call and twit him with a godly tract.
>
> \* \* \* \* \* \*

> I honestly confess that I would hinder
> The Scottish member's legislative rigs,
> Who looks on erring souls as straying pigs
> That must be lashed by law, wherever found,
> And driven to church as to the parish pound.'

Then follow these beautiful lines:

> 'Spontaneously to God should tend the soul,
> Like the magnetic needle to the Pole;
> But what were that intrinsic virtue worth,
> Suppose some fellow with more zeal than knowledge,
> Fresh from St. Andrew's College,
> Should nail the conscious needle to the north?'

Then comes an autobiographic gem of rare beauty and workmanship—a gem flashing forth a ray serene of the inner and holier life of Hood:

> 'The humble records of my life to search,
> I have not herded with mere pagan beasts;
> But sometimes I have "sat at good men's feasts,"
> And I have been "where bells have knolled to church."
> Dear bells! how sweet the sounds of village bells,
> When on the undulating air they swim!
> Now loud as welcomes! faint, now, as farewells!
> And trembling all about the breezy dells,
> As fluttered by the wings of Cherubim.'

This is followed by a solemn scorn for those whose only religion is one of words and not of deeds. He says:

> 'A man may cry "Church! Church!" at every word,
> With no more piety than other people—
> A daw's not reckoned a religious bird
> Because it keeps a-cawing from a steeple.'

Next in turn is a scathing line or two on spiritual pride

> 'Shun pride, O Rae!—whatever sort beside
> You take in lieu, shun spiritual pride!
> A pride there is of rank—a pride of birth,
> A pride of learning, and a pride of purse,

> A London pride—in short, there be on earth
> A host of prides, some better and some worse.
> But of all prides, since Lucifer's attaint,
> The proudest swells a self-elected saint.'

While the crown of the poem is a closing apostrophe to what Hood considers a truly religious life:

> 'Thrice blessed, rather, is the man with whom
> The gracious prodigality of nature,
> The balm, the bliss, the beauty, and the bloom,
> The bounteous providence in every feature,
> Recall the good Creator to His creature,
> Making all earth a fane, all heaven its dome!
> To *his* tuned spirit the wild heather-bells
>     Ring Sabbath knells;
> The jubilate of the soaring lark
>     Is chaunt of clerk;
> For Choir, the thrush and the gregarious linnet;
> The sod's a cushion for his pious want:
> And, consecrated by the heaven within it,
> The sky-blue pool a font.
> Each cloud-capped mountain is a holy altar;
>     An organ breathes in every grove;
>     And the full heart's a Psalter
> Rich in deep hymns of gratitude and love.'

Such was the deep, fervid, healthy religion of Hood—not creed, but character; not cant, but praise.

Another powerful, yet humorous, sermon that Hood preached was on the unutterable selfishness of those who, in the wondrous wave of mercantile prosperity marking the early part of this century, built up fabulous fortunes and sought thereby to ape the aristocracy. It is said now that the day of large fortunes is over—and for many reasons it is a good thing it is so. The day for money-worship, however, is not over, and one of the tendencies democracy is undoubtedly evincing is an undue reverence for the golden calf. In the days of Hood, however, money was the universal passport: to be rich was to be god-like—to be poor was to be accursed—poverty was the Englishman's hell. Carlyle, writing of these days, says: 'Hell generally signifies the infinite terror, the thing a man is infinitely afraid of, and shudders and shrinks from, struggling with his whole soul to escape from it. With Christians it is the infinite terror of being found guilty before the just Judge. With old Romans it was the terror not of Pluto, for whom probably they cared little, but of doing unworthily, doing unvirtuously, which was their word for unmanfully. And now what is it if you pierce through his cants—his oft-repeated hearsays, what he calls his worship and so forth—What is his hell after all these reputable, oft-repeated hearsays, what is it? With hesitation, with astonishment, I pronounce it to be the terror of not succeeding; of not making Money, fame, or some other figure in the world—chiefly of not making money. Is it not a somewhat singular hell?' So asks Carlyle, and we say in reply, It is a very singular hell indeed. Well, to show up the folly, the vanity, the selfishness, and the sin associated with, and growing out of, this abject worship of money, as well as the toadyism and foolery that follow in its train, Hood wrote the poem of 'Miss Kilmansegg and her Golden Leg.' In it he sketches the pedigree, birth, childhood, education, accident, marriage, misery, and death of a daughter born of wealthiest parents, and inheritress of a fabulous fortune. And yet what did wealth do for her? It did not give her happiness, it did not stave off accident, and when accident came it could not save the precious limb. It did not secure for her a pure and loving husband, nor happy home—nor did it save her from an ignominious death. Gold could purchase gold. As gold it multiplied, and mounted up towards heaven; but its weight eventually sank the one who carried it, and betrayed the one who loved it. The poem might reasonably and rightly be called 'The Nemesis of Wealth.'

In the first place, Hood tells us how her ancestors laid the basis of family wealth in the dark days of taxation and usury adopted for the raising of funds in the war times and Pitt administration. This ancestor, we are told, kept

> 'One yearling bull
> Worth all Smithfield-market full
> Of the golden bulls of Pope Gregory.
> \* \* \* \* \* \*
> Moreover, he had a Golden Ass,
> Sometimes at stall, and sometimes at grass,
> That was worth his own weight in money—
> And a golden hive, on a Golden Bank,
> Where golden bees, by alchemical prank,
> Gathered gold instead of honey.
> \* \* \* \* \* \*
> But the Golden Ass, or the Golden Bull,
> Was English John, with his pockets full,
> Then at war by land and water.
> \* \* \* \* \* \*
> And as money makes money, his golden bees
> Were the Five per Cents—or which you please.'

So the family fortune was laid, and so it was built up. The next generation, however, was more favoured (or more cursed), inheriting this fabulous wealth, with a power to multiply and keep it. To this generation was born a daughter —the heiress to the fortune—the heroine of the poem:

> 'She was born exactly at half-past two,
> As witnessed a timepiece in ormolu
> That stood on a marble table—

> Showing at once the time of day,
> And a team of Gildings running away
>   As fast as they were able,
> With a Golden God, with a golden Star,
> And a golden Spear, in a golden Car,
>   According to Grecian fable.'

Of course her christening was in keeping with her birth and position.

> 'A wealthy Nabob was God-papa,
> And an Indian Begum was God-mamma,
>   Whose jewels a queen might covet—
> And the priest was a Vicar, and Dean withal
> Of that temple we see with a Golden Ball,
>   And a Golden Cross above it.
>
> \*   \*   \*   \*   \*   \*
>
> Gold! still gold! it rained on the nurse,
> Who, unlike Danaë, was none the worse;
>   There was nothing but guineas glistening!
>   Fifty were given to Doctor James,
>     For calling the little Baby names,
>     And for saying "Amen"
>     The Clerk had ten,
> And that was the end of the Christening.'

Of her childhood, Hood tells us:

> 'Born in wealth, and wealthily nursed,
> Capp'd, papp'd, napp'd, and lapp'd from the first
>   On the knees of Prodigality,
> Her childhood was one eternal round
> Of the game of going on Tickler's ground,
>   Picking up gold—in reality.'

As for her education:

> 'Long before her A B and C,
> They had taught her by heart her L. S. D.
> And as how she was born a great heiress;

> And as sure as London is built of bricks,
> My Lord would ask her the day to fix,
> To ride in a fine gilt coach and six,
>   Like Her Worship the Lady May'ress.'

Thus are the children born to wealth too often and too early fooled. But, what was worse, her attendants mixed the alloy of gold with her morals; for:

> 'The very metal of merit they told,
> And praised her for being as "good as gold!"
>   Till she grew as a peacock haughty;
> Of money they talked the whole day round,
> And weighed desert like grapes by the pound,
> Till she had an idea from the very sound,
>   That people with naught were naughty.
>       \*     \*     \*     \*     \*     \*
> They praised her falls, as well as her walk,—
> Flatterers make cream cheese of chalk—
> They praised—how they praised!—her very small talk,
>   As if it fell from a Solon.'

Among other accomplishments, this heiress was taught the art of horseman- or horsewoman-ship; and here Hood's humour runs riot. The horse's name was 'Banker,' and it was of 'metal rare.' One day as he was carrying his mistress—his golden treasure—he shied—at what? At the 'sight of a beggar in rags.'

> 'Away went the horse in the madness of fright,
> And away went the horsewoman, mocking the sight—
> Was yonder blue flash a flash of blue light,
>   Or only the skirt of her habit?'

And now comes a description of the ride—as fine an example of imitative and descriptive writing as ever fell from pen, and only equalled by Browning in his galloping song, 'How they brought the good news from Ghent to Aix.'

'Away she gallops!—its awful work!
It's faster than Turpin's ride to York,
   On Bess, that notable clipper!
She has circled the ring!—she crosses the Park!
Mazeppa, although he was stripp'd so stark,
   Mazeppa could not outstrip her!
The fields seem running away with the folks!
The Elms are having a race for the Oaks
   At a pace that all jockies disparages!
All, all is racing! The Serpentine
Seems rushing past like the "arrowy Rhine,"
The houses have got on a railway line,
   And are off like the first-class carriages!
   \*    \*    \*    \*    \*    \*
Alas! for the hope of the Kilmanseggs!
For her head, her brains, her body, and legs,
   Her life's not worth a copper!
       Willy-nilly,
       In Piccadilly,
A hundred hearts turn sick and chilly,
   A hundred voices cry "Stop her!"
And one old gentleman stares and stands,
Shakes his head and lifts his hands,
   And says, "How very improper!"
   \*    \*    \*    \*    \*    \*
Sick with horror, she shuts her eyes,
But the very stones seem uttering cries,
   \*    \*    \*    \*    \*    \*
   "Batter her! Shatter her!
   Throw and scatter her"
Shouts each stony-hearted chatterer!
   "Dash at the heavy Dover!
Spill her, kill her, tear and tatter her!
Smash her! crash her!" (the stones didn't flatter her!)
"Kick her brains out! let her blood spatter her!
   Roll on her over and over."
   \*    \*    \*    \*    \*    \*
On and on! still frightfully fast!
Dover Street, Bond Street, all are past,

> But—yes—no—yes!—they are down at last!
> The Furies and Fates have found them!
> Down they go with a sparkle and crash,
> Like a bark that's struck by the lightning flash—
> There's a shriek—and a sob—
> And the dense, dark mob
> Like a billow closes around them.
>
> *  *  *  *  *  *
>
> "She breathes!"  "She don't!"
> "She'll recover!"  "She won't!"
> "She's stirring! she's living, by Nemesis!"'

She is at once removed into the nearest house, which happens to be 'an opulent goldsmith's premises.'

> 'But what avails gold to Miss Kilmansegg,
> When the femoral bone of her dexter leg
> Has met with a compound fracture?
>
> *  *  *  *  *  *
>
> Gold may soothe adversity's smart;
> Nay, help to bind up a broken heart;
> But to try it on any other part
> Were as certain a disappointment
> As if one should rub the dish and plate
> Taken out of a Staffordshire crate—
> In the hope of a golden service of state—
> With Singleton's Golden Ointment.'

In spite of all that gold could do, the leg had to be amputated. But how replaced? Ah! that was the question. An heiress must have a leg to match. A wooden leg? Pah! nothing so common.

> 'Wood, indeed, in forest and park,
> With its sylvan honours and feudal bark,
> Is an aristocratical article;
> But split and sawn, and hack'd about town,
> Serving all needs of pauper or clown,
> Trod on! staggered on! Wood cut down
> Is vulgar—fibre and particle.'

Well, if wood is too vulgar, what about cork? Could she not move gracefully with a neatly shaped limb of so light a material? No; worse and worse.

> 'Cork! When the noble Cork Tree shades
> A lovely group of Castilian maids,
>   'Tis a thing for a song and sonnet.
> But cork, as it stops the bottle of gin,
> Or bungs the beer—the *small* beer—in,
> It pierced her heart like a corking-pin
>   To think of standing upon it.'

No; she would have a leg of gold.

> 'So a leg was made in a comely mould,
> Of gold, fine virgin glittering gold,
>   As solid as man could make it—
> Solid in foot, and calf, and shank,
> A prodigious sum of money it sank,
> In fact, 'twas a Branch of the family Bank,
>   And no easy matter to break it.'

And now commenced her career of notoriety. Her fame spread far and wide; and so proud was she that she rested not until she had given a fancy ball, to which the nobility and plutocracy were invited, and in which the great show-object was the leg of gold. It is needless to follow her through the many intrigues formed to secure her hand—or rather, we should say, leg, for the golden limb was the attraction. At last she singled out a worthless foreign count, who married her, abused her, and finally brained her with the limb of gold, to her so precious, and to him so coveted, because by it he purposed to pay off his ever-accumulating debts.

Sad indeed is the ending of this unfortunate girl as depicted by Hood. She is not married for love, but bought for her wealth—her money bringing no happiness to the home, but only feeding the reckless and lustful habits of her husband. Night after night she sits alone in her gilded room, surrounded by her golden ornaments and her wealth of Midas. But there is no one to comfort her — no, not one. Her childhood—never the golden childhood of happiness, because so overshadowed with greed and selfishness—lies in the past. Her mother is hopelessly insane, her brain turned to imbecility by gold; and her father lies dead. Yet for these she weeps not. She rather weeps for very pride—pride wounded by the neglect of him whom she has made rich, and who repays her by his scorn and falsity. To whom can she turn? Alas! gold has separated her from all.

> 'But friend or gossip she had not one
> To hear the vile deeds that the Count had done,
>   How night after night he rambled;
> And how she had learned by sad degrees
> That he drank, and smoked, and worse than these,
>   That he swindled, intrigued, and gambled.'

So while gold purchases much, it loses much. It can win sycophancy, but it scatters sympathy. While it purchases flattery it sacrifices friends.

So enraged and mortified is this woman at her husband's treatment of her that she burns the will before his face, in which she has turned over her estates to him. As a revenge, and also because of a crying need of cash for his instant wants, he robs her of her limb in sleep, and as she wakes in alarm, dashes it down upon her head, her idol becoming her doom.

A terrible sermon from a terrible text to those who can read the truth between the lines of humour. While we laugh at the absurdity of the plot, we weep at the irony and tragedy hidden therein. The Nemesis of wealth! What avenging spirit more certain in its tread, more awful in its doom? 'Born to the world's wine, honey, and corn;' pampered in all the extravagance of affluence, trained in childhood to worship at the golden altar of a golden god, and to reverence the golden rule of cash rather than the golden rule of Christ. Taught her £ s. d. before her A B C, and morally debauched with flattering lips set loose with salve of gold. Courted, suited, sought after for what she had and not for what she was. And then to awaken to the terrible fact that her wealth could neither stave off accident nor mitigate misfortune; neither win a husband's heart nor a friend's solace; neither ease a proud spirit nor comfort a broken heart. And, worst of all, to be sacrificed upon a golden altar, herself the unwilling yet golden victim, the very death-blow given with that which in life she had hugged, and loved, and cherished. A picture this too often seen—a fact too frequently enacted. 'Go to, now, ye rich men, weep and howl for your miseries that shall come upon you. Your riches are corrupted and your garments are moth-eaten. Your gold and your silver is cankered, and shall eat into your flesh as it were fire. Ye have heaped up treasure together for the last days.'

Hood had a large heart, and was an intense lover of his kind. Suffering moved him, and by his poems he did much to lessen the pangs of the overworked and of the fallen. Indeed, almost all the social evils of the day received his sympathetic attention, and towards their amelioration he said and wrote much. The land and game laws were then, as now, a scandal; and it was with the purpose of showing up their inefficiency, and even their aggravation of the evil they pretended to cure, that he wrote 'The Lay of the Labourer,' in which occur the lines :

> 'Ay, only give me work,
>   And then you need not fear
> That I shall snare his worship's hare,
>   Or kill his grace's deer.
>
> \*    \*    \*    \*    \*    \*
>
> Wherever Nature needs,
>   Whenever Labour calls,
> No job I'll shirk of the hardest work,
>   To shun the workhouse walls ;
>
> \*    \*    \*    \*    \*    \*
>
> My only claim is this,
>   With labour stiff and stark,
> By lawful turn, my living to earn,
>   Between the light and dark :
> My daily bread, and nightly bed,
>   My bacon and drop of beer—
> But all from the hand that holds the land,
>   And none from the overseer.'

Hood stood up for the rights of the overworked, and showed how in many instances such overwork grew out of the thoughtlessness of the rich. This is strikingly set forth in the 'Lady's Dream,' where one of the high-born beauties is roused in the middle of the night by the tortured bodies of those who have had to toil to dress her in her robes, so rich and rare.

> 'And oh ! those maidens young,
>   Who wrought in that dreary room,
> With figures drooping and spectres thin,
>   And cheeks without a bloom :—
> And the Voice that cried—" For the pomp of pride
>   We haste to an early tomb.
>
> '" For the pomp and pleasure of Pride,
>   We toil like Afric's slaves,
> And only to earn a home at last

>     Where yonder cypress waves";—
>     And then they pointed,—I never saw
>     A ground so full of graves.
>
> \* \* \* \* \* \*
>
>     "Alas! I have walked thro' life
>         Too heedless where I trod;
>     Nay, helping to trample my fellow-worm,
>         And fill the burial sod—
>     Forgetting that even the sparrow falls
>         Not unmarked of God.
>
> \* \* \* \* \* \*
>
>     The wounds I might have heal'd!
>         The human sorrow and smart!
>     And yet it never was in my soul
>         To play so ill a part:
>     But evil is wrought by want of Thought
>         As well as want of Heart."'

'The Song of the Shirt,' a poem too well known to call for comment here, is of the same order, and has, in its own way, done much to free the many thousands of poor seamstresses from the tyranny of money-making masters. Though much yet remains to be done ere this curse of toil is removed, those who seek to lessen the evil return again and again to Hood for their inspiration; while 'The Bridge of Sighs' has done much towards rousing in the heart of Christendom a thought for the fallen and the unfortunate of our large cities.

Hood's tenderness was as marked as his humour. There are touches in his poems as gentle and as beautiful as any in the idylls of our own Laureate. For example, upon the death of his sister from consumption, he wrote:

>     'We watch'd her breathing thro' the night,
>         Her breathing soft and low,
>     As in her breast the wave of life
>         Kept heaving to and fro.

> 'So silently we seem'd to speak,
>   So slowly moved about,
> As we had lent her half our powers
>   To eke her living out.
>
> 'Our very hopes belied our fears,
>   Our fears our hopes belied—
> We thought her dying when she slept,
>   And sleeping when she died.
>
> 'For when the morn came dim and sad,
>   And chill with early showers,
> Her quiet eyelids closed—she had
>   Another morn than ours.'

There is also a psychological and dramatic instinct in Hood that calls for note. In 'Eugene Aram' and 'The Haunted House' we have betrayed an insight into conscience, and a weird, realistic touch that places Hood high above the mere comic school of poets. But, alas! he had to write to live; and he found that puns were the best preservatives against duns, for his publishers paid him for his rollicking mirth rather than for his graver and greater themes.

We have need to thank God for teachers such as Hood. Too many of those who instruct us leave behind in their instruction the sting of severity—they are too personal, too cynical, too severe. They portray our follies in high colours, they use a superabundance of vermilion and lampblack. In their schools we learn to loathe humanity, and look at ourselves in hopelessness and despair. Against these we have another school of teachers, who treat life as a huge joke. Their text is, 'A short life and a merry one, and a fig for care, and a sneer for sin.' They degrade all the moral element we possess by flippancy and ridicule, until righteousness and truth—nay, religion itself—become part and parcel of a fool's burlesque and a simpleton's fantasy. One class of teachers dress life in crape—the other don it with tinsel and cap and bells. To one it is a dirge, to the other drollery. The first dispirit us, the second debauch us. The former show us sins, and weight us with condemnation. The latter scoff at our sins, and so honeycomb our moral sense. Hood belonged to neither school. He saw sin, and he rebuked it; but he so rebuked it as not only to shame the sinner, but to inspirit him with hope and life. Wordsworth was sombre and stately in all rebukes he administered to his age and its sins. Byron was profane and immoral, and turned even the eternal verities of life into food for jest. But Hood combined Wordsworth's righteousness with Byron's jest. He often pointed a moral with a pun, and climaxed a sermon with a joke.

Then think of all the pleasure Hood has brought to us as an English-reading people. We hail the discoverer of a new drug, and look upon him as a benefactor of the race who, by introducing some anæsthetic, lessens pain and expedites surgery. We immortalize the man who invents a labour-saving and capital-increasing machine. But what of the man who, with his merry rhyme, and artless drollery, and innocent mirth, can dry the eye and cheer the heart, and lighten care, and gild the sombre cloud? who enables the harassed to forget their burden, and the sorrowful their despair? This is what Hood has done for us, and we acknowledge God in the gift. If there is one man to be pitied more than another, it is he who is a stranger to Lamb, to Thackeray, and to Hood, and others of their school, who, while themselves tormented and afflicted, sang the sweeter for their darkened cage, and sent forth rarer scents because their petals were bruised and torn. Lamb, shutting up in his heart the secret of his sister's insanity, and working night and day to keep her from the walls of a madhouse, and yet withal cheering the world with his 'Essays of Elia.' Thackeray, fighting with monetary difficulties, and the victim of an insidious disease, and yet, notwithstanding these, giving us his immortal creations, and delivering his humorous sketches—in reality sermons—a prince amongst the teachers of the day. And Hood—poor Hood!—wasted by constant hæmorrhage of the lungs, and flying from duns for the debts of those for whom he had become responsible, and in the pauses of his paroxysms, and in the pauses of his flight, throwing off the side-splitting stanza on the all too-comic phase of life. Ah! these are the men who have made life under all its horrible conditions tolerable—who have made literature a panacea for care and grief—who have so retouched the sombre horizon that the faded colours reappear, and the tints of hope and gladness start forth afresh.

We are loath to part with Hood—Hood the delicate, the simple-hearted, the gentle, tender, childlike Hood; merry in his misery and hopeful in his gloom; chivalrous towards women, irreproachable in his dealings with his fellow-men; wroth at injustice, merciful towards the fallen; the favourite of little children, the pet and playfellow of the best men of his age; the friend of all, the enemy of none. We can best bid him farewell in the words of Landor:

> 'Before me in each path there stood
> The witty and the tender Hood.'

# VI.

*TENNYSON, THE MOODIST.*

## VI.

## TENNYSON, THE MOODIST.

IN my definition of the characteristic of Tennyson's poetry I have ventured to coin the word 'moodist'—a word which however impermissible is none the less apposite. Tennyson is, undoubtedly, the poet of moods. He is in touch with every sensation common to the heart of man, woman, and child. He can pitch his poetry to any key in the gamut of feeling: —from monody to jubilate his note is true, his touch is perfect. Or to change the figure—he is familiar with the demons and the angels that people the soul, overshadowing it with mist, or irradiating it with glory; now stealing in uninvited, and remaining in spite of frantic efforts at dismissal; now refusing to linger when besought to remain with cries and prayers. Hate of man and hate of money, and love of woman and love of wealth. Scorn of sham and scorn of self; tears for the dead, and tears for the desolate. The maddened wail of disappointment, the wild cry of revenge, the heart-sob of the mother, the sad retrospect of the grandmother, the childish delight on a bright May day, the gloomy ghost of doubt, the mute shadow of grief, the rollicking carouser, the spectre of lust haunting a heart worn out and gray with dying fires, the well-conditioned, yet chilly self-centred god in the Palace of Art, the yearning, passionate lonesomeness of a forsaken wife—all these, and many more of the phantoms, passions, and moods, by which mankind is visited, are no strangers to him, and to these he introduces us in his poems. It is as though Tennyson had thrown all human hearts, in all their mad passions and gruesome griefs, in all their wild excitements and passionate joys, into life-pictures on the walls of some great gallery, and bidden the spectators (or readers of his poems) to look at them, and behold the moods of the souls of men. Next to the Bible and Shakespeare, I know of no writings so full, so true, so startling in their revelation of moods as the writings or poems of Tennyson.

Thus it is important for those who mean to appreciate Tennyson to put themselves, as far as they can, in the place and in the spirit of the characters whom the poet describes; and also, as far as possible, to enter into the temper, or shade of temper (for Tennyson is fine even to shades), peculiar to the time, the place, and the personality. In a word, the student of Tennyson, like the student of Shakespeare, must be a student of human nature. I claim this as a *sine quâ non* for a right appreciation of the Laureate. Apart from this you may admire his chaste and superbly finished style, his pictorial genius in the setting forth of landscape, his pre-Raphaelite touch, peculiar to his vignette sketches, and his marvellous power of condensation, saying in a line, as Ruskin puts it, what it takes a first-class author a page or a page and a half to express. All these striking features, each distinct and pre-eminent in his writings, you may admire; but only they who are students of the human heart, its passions, its aspirations, its disappointments, and its gloom, can truly and fairly appreciate Tennyson, the poet of moods.

Now what is a mood? It is a soul experience or sensation, resultant from one of two causes, or, it may be, from both. For example, we bring into this world with us a certain mental or psychologic atmosphere—an atmosphere, for the most part, in which we live and move and have our being. Such atmosphere may be rarefied or intensified as the case may be; this being consequent upon circumstances and conditions. Say, a man brings with him into the world the spirit of jealousy. He may be a good man, a considerate man, even a self-sacrificing man; but he is always plagued and fretted by this atmosphere of jealousy. When rivals press him the cloud thickens, and the vapours fall. When they are removed from immediate contact, although the sky clears, the clouds still curl in their coppery folds along the distant horizon. More or less the thing is there —either in murk or haze—in blackness or in falling shadow. As with jealousy, so with a hundred other passions and crazes. We are belted with a moral atmosphere, ever changing in rarity and colour, according to the hour, the place, the circumstance. Thus our souls move as orbs through an ever-varying medium; all within them taking tone from the all-encompassing and ever-pressing mood.

This mental-atmosphere is Tennyson's world. It seems as though he had visited it in a thousand souls, and knew it in all its manifold changes. For example, take the following as setting forth the mood of hate and thickening into the passion-storm of cruel, deadly revenge. The poem is entitled 'The Sisters,' and it consists of six verses of four lines, each verse relieved with two lines of a refrain that rise in passion as the storm outside the castle increases in fury.

The plot is as follows :—A young earl of great beauty wooes a girl, and then seduces and deserts her. She dies of a broken heart, while the elder sister, once the earl's betrothed, and who had withdrawn in favour of the younger, whom he loved more than herself,, determines upon a plan of revenge—relentless, unwomanly, and hellish. She insinuates herself into his affections, decoys him to her couch, lulls him to sleep, stabs him dead, and lays his bloody corpse at his mother's feet. I want you to note the rise of this woman's passion, with the rise of the storm—the mood of the soul and the mood of nature keeping pace, and tune, and strength together.

> ' We were two daughters of one race :
> She was the fairest in the face :
>   The wind is blowing in turret and tree.
> They were together, and she fell ;
> Therefore revenge became me well.
>   O the earl was fair to see !
>
> ' She died : she went to burning flame :
> She mixed her ancient blood with shame.
>   The wind is howling in turret and tree.
> Whole weeks and months, and early and late,
> To win his love I lay in wait ;
>   O the earl was fair to see !
>
> ' I made a feast ; I bade him come ;
> I won his love, I brought him home.
>   The wind is roaring in turret and tree.
> And after supper, on a bed,
> Upon my lap he laid his head ;
>   O the earl was fair to see !
>
> ' I kiss'd his eyelids into rest :
> His ruddy cheeks upon my breast.
>   The wind is raging in turret and tree.
> I hated him with the hate of hell,
> But I loved his beauty passing well.
>   O the earl was fair to see !

'I rose up in the silent night:
I made my dagger sharp and bright.
   The wind is raving in turret and tree.
As half asleep his breath he drew,
Three times I stabbed him thro' and thro'.
   O the earl was fair to see!

'I curled and combed his comely head,
He looked so grand when he was dead.
   The wind is blowing in turret and tree.
I wrapped his body in the sheet,
And laid him at his mother's feet.
   O the earl was fair to see!'

After all, the poem is but the elder sister's dream; yet it is the dream of hate intensified to revenge—a mood of the soul.

Another poem portraying soul-moods is 'The Palace of Art.' It unfolds the tempers of selfishness and self-renouncement—of isolation, ending in despair, and universal sympathy, crowned with joy. In the former temper the soul proposes to itself a life of gratification, and we are introduced to its intentions and doings in the following lines:

'I built my soul a lordly pleasure-house,
   Wherein at ease for aye to dwell.
I said, "O Soul, make merry and carouse,
   Dear soul, for all is well."'

Then, in graphic sketches, Tennyson gives us the position, the prospect, and the surroundings of the Palace. The site selected is 'far away from, and far above, the world of toiling men,' built upon 'a huge crag platform, smooth as burnished brass.' The outlook is upon 'level meadow bases of deep grass,' while the scenes and sounds of the great sea of life—its wrecks and storms—are shut out by 'bright ranged ramparts, which rise and scale the light.'

These sheltered quarters of the selfish soul are laid out in richest luxuriance. 'Floods of fountain foam' are poured from the golden throats of cisterns forged in the forms of dragons, which stand at the four angles of the Palace, the currents of these uniting in one mighty stream, which, rushing over the mountain-side, scatters clouds of spray, on which the sunbeams paint the rainbow arch; while beyond lies the sapphire sea.

The poet then proceeds to sketch the interior of the Palace. The rooms are hung with richest draperies, and the walls relieved with finished works of art. The fittings are of deep-wrought wood, the niches of which are filled with the statuettes of saviours, martyrs, and patriots of all ages. The roof is a mighty angel with outstretched wings; the floor a marvellous mosaic, representative of the struggling, toiling, forsaken, and perishing races of men. Within this costly home the selfish soul shuts herself up from all her kind, and lives alone, away from sight and sound of suffering, as well as from the call and appeal of duty. Then Tennyson proceeds to outline the selfish mood.

> 'She took her throne:
> She sat betwixt the shining Oriels,
> To sing her songs alone.'

And

> 'Singing and murmuring in her feastful mirth,
>   Joying to feel herself alive,
> Lord over Nature, Lord of the visible earth,
>   Lord of the senses five;
> Communing with herself: "All these are mine,
>   And let the world have peace or wars,
> 'Tis one to me."
>
> \*　　\*　　\*　　\*　　\*　　\*
>
> O God-like isolation which art mine,
>   I can but count thee perfect gain,

\* \* \* \* \* \*
I take possession of man's mind and deed.
I care not what the sects may brawl.
I sit as God, holding no form of creed,
But contemplating all."'

For some time the selfish soul draws joy from this isolation, shelter, and æsthetic environment. Eventually, however, she is troubled with strange questionings—questionings that press in upon her from the world without, despite her withdrawal and distance therefrom:

' Full oft the riddle of the painful earth
Flashed thro' her as she sat alone,
Yet not the less held she her solemn mirth,
And intellectual throne.
And so she throve and prosper'd; so three years
She prosper'd—on the fourth she fell.'

Yes! she fell—and how great that fall the poet proceeds to depict. In a dream, as when one awaketh, so suddenly and precipitately, came the collapse. The Palace is changed to a tomb; the kingdom of her contemplation passes into wildest confusion; solitude, once so sweet, is unbearable; and the much-sought-after and hardly-earned isolation is turned into a hell. Uncertain shapes start from out the void that belts her, ' white-eyed phantasms weeping tears of blood,' human forms, their foreheads fretted deep with care, their hearts alight with flame, baby corpses, stark and staring, reared against the crumbling walls—these being meant by the poet to represent all who had been allowed to perish unhelped and unheeded by the neglect and isolation of the selfish soul. Yes! the sick whom she might have visited, the naked whom she might have clothed, the hungry whom she might have fed, now rise up against her to torment and condemn her. Thus Tennyson paints the hell to which every self-seeking and self-centred life is doomed. I cannot help here inserting in passing the words of Ruskin: 'They who are begrudging of their means, and store it up from others, find ere long that, like the manna kept in the wilderness tent, it doth naught but stink and breed worms.'

Tennyson goes on to show that the suffering through which this selfish soul is passing is punitive rather than vindictive in its character. She soon cries out:

'"I am on fire within."
 There comes no murmur of reply.
"What is it that will take away my sin,
 And save me lest I die?"
\* \* \* \* \* \*
So when four years were wholly finished,
 She threw her royal robes away.
"Make me a cottage in the vale," she said,
 "Where I may mourn and pray.
Yet pull not down my palace towers, that are
 So lightly, beautifully built:
Perchance I may return with others there
 When I have purged my guilt."'

Note the word 'others.' She would for ever live in the cottage and in the vale rather than return alone to her Palace of Art. Her punishment has taught her the greatest of all life's lessons, that to live well and to live happily we must live for others. Not that the Palace need be pulled down. No! The sin was in neither its costliness nor its beauty. It was the selfishness of the occupant that cursed it. She sought to break the God-forged link, 'Ye are members one of another.' She sought to reverse the God-made law, 'He that would save his life must lose it.' She wanted to possess life's pleasures without sharing them, to live disintegrated from her kind. For this end she removed herself from the world, and enshrined herself with all that heart, fancy, and genius could imagine. And with what consequence? The ruin of her nature, the distress of her soul.

Thus it is with every soul that severs itself from its fellow-souls. Like the shallow pool, left high by the receding tide, it can know no freshness, no sweetness, no fulness, until once more gathered into the great tidal ocean which is its native source. Only as we find room in our hearts and homes for others can we enter into the true purpose of being. 'Except the Lord build the house they labour in vain that build it.'

'Locksley Hall,' the poem I consider Tennyson's masterpiece, is another swiftly moving panorama of moods. An orphaned youth, poor, yet highly gifted, seeks the hand of his heiress-cousin Amy, whose father, the squire, owns the broad acres of Locksley, in Lincolnshire. This squire opposes the match, forcing his child into wedlock with a scion of the aristocracy; whereupon her disconsolate and rejected cousin enlists in the army, and seeks relief upon the field of battle. Here, despite his reckless deeds, he remains unhurt, and lives to return with his regiment to the old land. As chance would have it, the regiment in marching to barracks-quarters takes the turn-pike, from which is caught a glimpse of Locksley Hall, the scene of his early love and sorrow. Old thoughts and associations come rushing back upon him, old wounds are torn open, and he is, for the moment, unmanned with reminis-cences of the past. He asks his comrades to leave him for a short time in the rear while he again surveys the once loved, and now long forsaken, spot. The same old hall; the same waste of moorland, with its dreary gleams and calling curlews, and distant roar of hollow breaking waves. He sees the ivied casement-windows from which, in the days of boyhood, he used to watch the stars and the level stretches of beach along which he was wont to study history and science. Then the ghost of his lost Amy flits before him—Amy, tender-hearted, with her pale and delicate cheek, that flushed as with the 'rosy red' of the northern night at the mention of his love. Next follows his remembrance of the delirium of love's young dream, when

'Love took up the glass of Time, and turned it in his glowing hands;
Every moment, lightly shaken, ran itself in golden sands.
Love took up the harp of Life, and smote on all the chords with might;
Smote the chord of Self, that, trembling, passed in music out of sight.'

But, alas! Amy was shallow-hearted—she was false and fickle. She yielded to her father's threats, and quailed before her mother's tongue, as they twain bade her forsake an impoverished cousin for the hand of a wealthy lord. And now commences the series of moods through which the wronged and disappointed man passes as he looks at her with the eye of fancy, and compares what he deems she may be with what she might have been had she married him. Can he wish her happiness, seeing she has thus thrown herself away? Did she not in that act decline to a range of lower feeling and to a narrower heart? Has she not, through her union with mere wealth and rank and animalism, sunk to their level, 'all within her growing coarse to sympathize with clay'? for

'As the husband is, the wife is: thou art mated with a clown,
And the grossness of his nature will have weight to drag thee down.

He will hold thee, when his passion shall have spent its novel force,
Something better than his dog, a little dearer than his horse.'

Then, swift as passing cloud, the mood changes, and he dwells with passionate denunciation upon the causes of his failure to gain her heart and retain her love. He was without social rank, without worldly means, without fine polish of manners ; and wanting these his manliness and truthfulness and pure spontaneous devotion went for nought, and he cries :

' Cursed be the social wants that sin against the strength of youth !
Cursed be the social lies that warp us from the living truth !
Cursed be the sickly forms that err from honest Nature's rule !
Cursed be the gold that gilds the straitened forehead of the fool !'

And now he passes to another mood—a quieter and more reflective one. He asks himself if it is well he should thus bluster and rave ? Is he not mad to cherish that which bears such bitter fruit ? Will it not be wiser to forget—to wash the tablets of his memory in the waters of oblivion ? But he cannot. In vain he looks for the sweet, oblivious antidote. To forget is impossible—the past is indelibly stamped upon his heart. Then he tries to find comfort in the divisions of the mind—that is, he dwells upon the sunny rather than upon the gloomy past. He will part Amy from her self, taking that portion of her life which she lived when she was his, and when she loved him. But, on a moment's reflection, he finds he cannot because she never loved him truly. If she had, she would still have loved him, ' for love is love for evermore.'

Then there passes before him, like a vision in the night, the awful blight of a pure woman linked to the man who is nothing more in tastes and tendencies than a brute-beast.

It is the dead, unhappy night; the rain beats upon the roof, while she lies with sleepless eye staring at the chamber-wall whereon the dying night-lamp flickers, and the shadows rise and fall, while upon the marriage-pillow her husband sleeps off his drunken orgie. Surely, now her thoughts will turn to her old love, to her true love, to him whom she cast off, and who would never thus have outraged her modesty and womanhood? Surely, now she will see his eye looking ancient kindness, and think of 'the might have beens.' No. He cannot even hope for solace here, for a babe is born to her, and this new life not only helps to bring her solace, but altogether crowds the old love out of her memory. And here come the beautiful lines:

'Nay, but Nature brings thee solace; for a tender voice will cry.
'Tis a purer life than thine; a lip to drain thy trouble dry.
Baby lips will laugh me down; my latest rival brings thee rest.
Baby fingers, waxen touches, press me from the mother's breast.'

Again the mood changes. He passes from the passive to the active. He will brood no longer, but seek solace in the activities of life:

'Overlive it—lower yet—be happy! Wherefore should I care?
I myself must mix with action, lest I wither by despair.'

But to what is he to turn? He is poor, and the gates of advance open only to the golden key; and what is more, they are thronged with suitors; all the world's market-places are crowded. Well, then, he will try to relive his life. He will seek once more to feel the wild pulsation which he felt before the strife—when he yearned for the large excitement that coming years would yield—when he looked out with the eye of hope, and beheld a propitious future—when he pictured in no fancy, but as a near reality, the parliament of man and the federation of the world. But, alas! wherein lies the uses of recalling old aspirations? They were only the political dream of his youth, shattered long since by revolution and civil strife.

At this moment the bugle sounds for his return, and with the sounding bugle the mood again changes. This time it is the mood of scorn—scorn at his own folly to thus fret and fume over a woman's fickleness and falsity:

> 'Weakness to be wrath with weakness! Woman's pleasure, woman's pain—
> Nature made them blinder motions bounded in a shallower brain:
> Woman is the lesser man, and all thy passions, match'd with mine,
> Are as moonlight unto sunlight, and as water unto wine.'

Once more the mood changes. He will go back to the old civilizations of the East—he will wander towards the gateways of the day—he will dwell in lands where no trader comes—where no European flag floats—where there is neither steamship nor railway, nor any of those thought-problems that shake mankind:

> 'There the passions, cramp'd no longer, shall have scope and breathing-space;
> I will take some savage woman, she shall rear my dusky race.'

And then, in a moment, he passes into a better mood:

> 'Fool, again the dream, the fancy! but I *know* my words are wild.
> But I count the gray barbarian lower than the Christian child.
> I, to herd with narrow foreheads, vacant of our glorious gains,
> Like a beast with lower pleasures, like a beast with lower pains!'

And now the mood brightens and heightens. He sees, after all, a beacon in the distance. Not eastward, but westward, moves the world, and fifty years of Europe are better than a cycle of Cathay. Therefore, farewell to Locksley

Hall, and farewell to Amy. The past is irrevocable; the future is sure and filled with promise.

> 'Forward, forward, let us range.
> Let the great world spin for ever down the ringing grooves of change.'

I call that poem a gorgeous panorama of moods—moods common to the disappointed and dispirited mind. Every phase of despair and every phase of hope are flashed before our eyes, until at last, with cry of 'onward,' 'forward,' 'duty,' 'work,' the victorious mood is reached out of which ascends the man.

And now we come to 'In Memoriam,' another mighty panorama of moods, only the moods are those of grief and loss—the moods benighting and fogging a bereaved soul. I need scarcely pause to remark that the poem is a monument in verse erected by Tennyson to the memory of the friend of his youth, Arthur Henry Hallam, who died an early death while in search of health in distant lands. It has not only immortalized the name of him to whom it was erected, but it has immortalized him who erected it. It is one of England's great classics. Religion and philosophy, science and art, are wrought into its verse like a glorious mosaic. It is a biography of Hallam, an autobiography of Tennyson, a revelation of the soul-experience of humanity under the shadow of loss, as well as a repertory of the doubts and faiths of the age.

You must remember, then, that 'In Memoriam' is a bereaved man's pilgrimage and progress from loss and doubt to reunion and faith. In the first stage of grief the lone sufferer falls back upon the old faith, that men may rise on stepping-stones of their dead selves to higher things; but when he comes to test the value of this principle in the face of the great loss under whose shadow he stands, he fails to find in it a gain to match. Out of Hallam's death, and his own broken heart, he can find no stepping-stone to higher things. But one thing is possible. He can keep his memory as a shrine whereat to worship, and so continue to love his dear dead friend. In order to do this he will nurse his grief, so that the lost in form shall never be the lost in thought.

> 'Let Love clasp Grief lest both be drown'd;
> Let darkness keep her raven gloss;
> Ah, sweeter to be drunk with loss,
> To dance with death, to beat the ground,
>
> Than that the victor hours should scorn
> The long results of love, and boast,
> "Behold the man that loved and lost,
> But all he was is overworn."'

Soon, however, the sympathy of friends is showered upon the poet in his bereavement. Kindly words and letters of condolence come from far and near, all well meant, but bringing nothing of cheer or comfort.

> 'One writes, that "Other friends remain,
> That Loss is common to the race,"—
> And common is the common place,
> And vacant chaff well meant for grain.
>
> 'That loss is common would not make
> My own less bitter, rather more;
> Too common! Never morning wore
> To evening, but some heart did break.'

The poet continues to feed and nurse his grief until all nature is seen through its solemn gloom. The once-peaceful surroundings of life lose their charm, the old scenes and associations are beclouded, because Hallam is no longer there to share them with him.

> 'So find I every pleasant spot
>   In which we two were wont to meet,
>   The field, the chamber, and the street,
> For all is dark, where thou art not.'

At last the burden of his grief is unbearable. The channels of relief in words and tears are choked. Like the old Hebrew poet, 'He is so troubled that he cannot speak. His eyes are held waking.' This mood he has faultlessly portrayed in the following lines:

> 'The lesser griefs that may be said,
>   That breathe a thousand tender vows,
>   Are but as servants in a house
> Where lies the master newly dead;
>
> 'Who speak their feeling as it is,
>   And weep the fulness from the mind:
>   "It will be hard," they say, "to find
> Another service such as this."
>
> 'My lighter moods are like to these,
>   That out of words a comfort win;
>   But there are other griefs within,
> And tears that at their fountain freeze.
>
> 'For by the hearth the children sit,
>   Cold in that atmosphere of Death,
>   And scarce endure to draw the breath,
> Or like to noiseless phantoms flit.
>
> 'But open converse is there none,
>   So much the vital spirits sink,
>   To see the vacant chair, and think,
> "How good! how kind! and he is gone."'

At last the gloom of sorrow is somewhat relieved. There is the subtle influence of the past at work. Is not he, Tennyson, a better and a holier man for having once had Hallam as a friend and guide? Does not the memory of Hallam still exert itself over him and companion him? Is there not the posthumous immortality of influence? To this he will cling, and rejoice in the fact that it is 'better to have loved and lost than never to have loved at all.'

But soon there dawns upon him another immortality—the immortality of his soul—the personality of Hallam—that which thought and loved and hoped—that in Hallam after which Tennyson was drawn, and to which Tennyson was attached. This it is impossible for death to touch; and although unseen, yet it is none the less real and near.

> 'My own dim life should teach me this,
>   That life shall live for evermore,
>   Else earth is darkness at the core,
> And dust and ashes all that is.'

And now the gloom of despair is changed to the dawn of hope. Death does not end all—it is rather the Spirit's bridal day—the hour of those nuptials when the soul of man is linked in celestial wedlock to the Lord of Life. And just as it behoves the bride to forsake father and mother and home, to take upon herself the higher and holier duties of a new sphere of life, so it was needful that Hallam should pass from earthly scenes and companionships, through the gate of death, to the bridal morn and marriage-feast, awaiting him in the heavenlies beyond. Realizing this, Tennyson sings:

> 'And, doubtless, unto thee is given
>   A life that bears immortal fruit,
>   In those great offices that suit
> The full-grown energies of heaven.'

Then Tennyson realizes another and grander truth, viz., that it was God's need of Hallam's power of usefulness in other worlds that led to his all too early removal:

> 'So many worlds, so much to do,
>   So little done, such things to be,
>   How know I what had need of thee?
> For thou wert strong as thou wert true.

Thus death is not only a gain to Hallam, it is a gain also to other worlds and to other intelligences; while in the end it is also a gain to the poet, his bereaved friend, for out of the suffering has come the purified and thoughtful mind, as he cries:

> 'Forgive my grief for one removed,
>   Thy creature, whom I found so fair.
>   I trust he lives in Thee, and there
> I find him worthy to be loved.'

Verily tribulation worketh patience, and patience experience, and experience hope—a hope that maketh not ashamed.

This is but the barest outline of the poem—a key only, with which I trust in your spare moments you will seek to unlock the doors of its many treasures.

'Maud,' rather than a panorama, is a rapid succession of tempestuous moods. The poem is a monologue, discovering a heart, in turn soured by life's failures, delirious with love's passions, maddened by poverty's limitations, burdened by blood-shedding remorse, and eventually emancipated by uniting itself with a world-reforming scheme, alike divine in its purpose and assured of its end. The monologist is the son and only child of a man who has lost all through a speculation into which he was fraudulently led, and who, to ease his aching heart, and escape his disgraced record, sought surcease in an act of self-destruction. He was soon followed to his untimely grave by his sorrowing and despondent wife, the boy alone remaining, a prey to 'the slings and arrows of outrageous fortune.' Tennyson introduces him to us while wrapped in the mood of cynicism and raillery. Looking out upon the world, he sees nothing but shammery and selfishness. The age is wrong, is false, is belittled by its passion for ill-gotten and ill-spent gain. 'Only the ledger lives, and only not all men lie.' Food is adulterated, and drink is drugged; the thief is abroad, discoverable alike in the stealthy marauder of the night and in the wage-oppressing capitalist. All this, however, he is asked to forget in the fact that the era of peace has dawned. *Era of peace, forsooth!* When the poor are hovelled and hustled together, each sex like swine—when a mammonite mother kills her babe for a burial-fee—when men care only for factory, counter, and till? Bah! such peace is a thousand times worse than war. Thus he grows weary and sickened with all things, even with his old love—his child-love—Maud, who is about to return, after years of education and travel, to the Hall on the hill. What will she care for him now that fortune has frowned upon him? What does he want with her now that all a woman counts dear has been withdrawn? No. Even against her he will close the door of his heart, and 'busy himself in himself while the devil pipes to his own.'

His next mood opens with an endeavour after a philosophic calm, broken by a glimpse of the beautiful Maud. He has *seen* her with her cold and clean-cut face, and downcast eye; but it is only a passing glance, and he congratulates himself upon escaping heart-free, with 'the least little touch of spleen.' He sees her again, however. This time to be sensitive to her surpassing beauty. She breaks like a star on his gloom profound; she grows and fades and grows upon his imagination, holding his eyes from sleep, and driving him to seek solace without the confines of himself and home. A third time he sees her, when she wafts him a sign of recognition; and then, sitting in the quiet of his own garden, he hears her voice stealing forth in song as she sings a martial strain beneath the cedar-tree in the meadow under the Hall.

In these successive sights, and in this climax of sound, Tennyson subtly traces out the development of the love-moods in the man's nature: in other words, we have in these musings and melancholies a revelation of the progressive stages of a heart in its love-ascent from the soured cynic that looks out upon a dead world to the awakened man that sees its light and glory.

The next mood is that in which his passion craves for contact, direct and personal. He must meet her face to face, and talk over with her the days of long ago. To this end he journeys forth in the wannish glare of a pale and stormy morning, only to be disappointed, for Maud remains within the shelter of the Hall. At evening, however, when the sunset burns on the blossomed gables of the cottages, and he, once more restless for her presence, wanders down the village street, they meet, touch hands, and talk of times gone by.

And now follow, in marvellous rapidity and graphic faithfulness, the varying and tormenting moods of one who stands midway between an all-absorbing passion and uncertainty as to its reciprocity on the part of the woman he loves. First, there is a suspicion: what if her smile were a snare to entrap and prostrate him at her feet, only that she might the more ignominiously spurn after she had befooled him: what if it were a trick to secure his vote at the county contest, where her brother is to stand as candidate; or worse, what if it were only the pitying smile of womanhood, started by sentimental thoughts as to his orphanhood, his poverty, and his isolation?

Then succeeds the mood of pride. Supposing Maud should love him! Will not her brother—'the jewelled mass of millinery,' oiled and curled, smelling of musk and insolence—will not he oppose the troth? Yet, after all, who is he that he should? To be scorned by one that we scorn is not a matter to make us fret—is not a calamity hard to be borne.

But there follows a mood that *is* hard to be borne—the mood of jealousy; for now comes upon the scene the new-made lord, before whom the villagers doff their hats, and who inherits untold wealth from an old grandfather, just dead, and gone to a blacker pit than the shafts of coal out of which he dug his wealth at the sacrifice of the helots he employed. He is rich ' in the grace all women desire,' and strong in 'the power all men adore.' A formidable rival, he, with his simper and drawl, his gewgaw castle and his modern title. How dares he to press in upon the presence of Maud—the darling of his heart—his loved one?

Gradually this love-passion becomes all-absorbing; he cannot withdraw from it, and all he hears and sees is leavened by it. As the birds sing in the falling twilight, their cry and call is 'Maud—Maud—Maud!' As he crosses the meadows in her wake, the tread of her feet gives a deeper crimson to the daisy-tips. Then the shadow falls, for 'my lord's' horse stands at the Hall front; his rival is kneeling at the shrine.

Upon the departure of this rival with her brother, our hero determines to press his suit. To this end Fortune is propitious, for he sees her approaching; whereat he cries:

> 'I see my Oread coming down,
> O this is the day!

> O beautiful creature, what am I
> That I dare to look her way;
> Think I may hold dominion sweet,
> Lord of the pulse that is lord of her breast,
> And dream of her beauty with tender dread,
> From the delicate Arab arch of her feet
> To the grace that, bright and light as the crest
> Of a peacock, sits on her shining head,
> And she knows it not: O, if she knew it,
> To know her beauty might half undo it.
> I know it the one bright thing to save
> My yet young life in the wilds of Time,
> Perhaps from madness, perhaps from crime,
> Perhaps from a selfish grave.'

They meet; he pleads his love. She yields, and in promise becomes his own.

And now all is changed. A new heaven and a new earth, because a goddess reigns therein. He sees all through the rainbow colours of love. He asks:

> 'Has our whole earth gone nearer to the glow
> Of your soft splendours that you look so bright?
> *I* have climbed nearer out of lonely Hell.
> Beat, happy stars, timing with things below,
> Beat with my heart more blest than heart can tell.'

All too soon the brother returns; and when informed by Maud in girlish hints of the affections of her heart, he first laughs her down, eventually frowning, and forbidding her to speak further with her betrothed. Thus their love-greetings and trysts are intercepted; yet Maud remains true, though she seeks to retain her sisterly duties side by side with the plight of love.

It so happens that this brother—the 'ponderous squire,' as he is called in the poem—gives a grand political dinner to half the squirelings of the neighbourhood, to follow with a dance for the maids and marriage-makers, where Maud is to appear in her jewels. It goes without saying our hero remains uninvited. At nightfall, however, he steals down to Maud's garden in the grounds of the Hall, where she meets him—meets him in her fairy attire, resplendent in her jewels and her budding youth. And yet, scarcely have they met, before her brother, who has been an unseen watcher, approaches, and accuses his sister's lover of trickery and ungentlemanliness in the urging and carrying out of his suit. This is indignantly denied, when, for reply, our hero receives a blow. Bad blood is now uppermost, and in return he fells his lover's brother with the stroke of Cain. 'Fly, fly!' was the dying man's cry. 'The fault was mine.'

And now the mood changes, as he flies before the minions of justice, bearing the murderer's brand, to the Breton coast. A deadlier gloom settles down upon him; not the former gloom of the man who has been wronged, but the more terrible gloom of the man who himself has perpetrated the wrong, and played the aggressor's part. On a foreign strand he sits and plucks the harmless field-flowers; but his hand is guilty—with that hand he plucked the life from the brother of Maud. He walks by the shore, and looks upon the 'tiny shells, forlorn' and void of their 'living will'; so Maud, like 'the empty cell,' has neither brother nor lover, and all through his own rash deed. He listens to the roar of ocean, and hears it thunder of wrecks and spoil. Alas! he of all wrecks is the greatest and saddest—a shipwrecked man on 'a coast of ancient fable and fear.' He raises his eye, but the horizon is ever darkened by the phantom of Maud. There she is, flitting to and fro, as 'his restless eyeballs roll.' Is it a disease— a mechanic ghost—a juggle of the brain? Why do all his surroundings awaken the deed of death? Why do flower and shell and sea all awaken reminiscences of the act of sin?

Then comes the hope—Is he dead! Was he not only stunned? May he not be living, and he himself only self-accused and innocent? And if this be so, may not Maud still love him? and may he not be reunited to her?

But alas! there comes again the phantom:

> 'It leads me forth at evening,
> It lightly winds and steals
> In a cold white robe before me,
> When all my spirit reels
> At the shouts, the leagues of lights,
> And the roaring of the wheels.'

It leads him back to a happy past:

> "'Tis a morning pure and sweet,
> And a dewy splendour falls
> On the little flower that clings
> To the turrets and the walls;
> 'Tis a morning pure and sweet,
> And the light and shadow fleet;
> She is walking in the meadow,
> And the woodland echo rings;
> In a moment we shall meet;
> She is singing in the meadow,
> And the rivulet at her feet
> Ripples on in light and shadow
> To the ballad that she sings.
>
> Do I hear her sing as of old,
> My bird with the shining head,
> My own dove with the tender eye?
> '*But there rings on a sudden a passionate cry,
> There is some one dying or dead.*'\*

Then all changes. A sudden thunder rolls, and the dream is broken. He goes forth, 'the death-like type of pain.' The eavedrops fall; the yellow vapours hang low,

\* Italics ours.

and choke the awakening city; the dull red sun is wrapped in drifts of lurid smoke. He goes forth, through the hubbub of the market, but the shadow is still there.

> 'But the broad light glares and beats,
> And the shadow flits and fleets
> And will not let me be;
> And I loathe the squares and streets,
> And the faces that one meets,
> Hearts with no love for me;
> Always I long to creep
> Into some still cavern deep,
> There to weep, and weep, and weep,
> My whole soul out to thee.'

This mood is followed by one of utter hopelessness. He is as though he were dead; with this exception, however, that, though dead, he cannot rest—though buried to everything, *he lies not deep enough.* He can hear the wheels go over his head, while his bones are shaken with the pain, the very horses beating with their hoofs into his scalp and brain:

> 'Driving, hurrying, marrying, burying,
> Clamour and rumble, and ringing and clatter,
> And here, beneath it all, as bad,
> For I thought the dead had peace, but it is not so;
> To have no peace in the grave—is that not sad?'

And now the railing mood of early days returns, but intensified a hundred-fold. The statesman betrays his party secret: the physician blabs the case of his patient. No man thinks for the public good. All is babble and cackle; confidence is betrayed for money or for gossip; all, all is rottenness, corruption, and sham.

Then we come to the closing, and, as Tennyson always has it, the triumphant mood. When, after weary years of creeping on with broken wing, through cells of madness and haunts of fear, the spring again returns, with its dewy downs and shining daffodils, he hears of a coming strife. As the months run on, this rumour of battle grows, and the armaments are ramped while he stands

> 'On a giant deck and mixed his breath
> With a loyal people shouting a battle-cry,'

and he himself awakes to the better mind; for

> 'It is better to fight for the good than rail at the ill;
> I have felt with my native land. I am one with my kind;
> I embrace the purpose of God, and the doom assigned.'

Thus Tennyson takes us through the four great stages in the development of a man. Starting with a soured and selfish nature, he finds surcease in an isolated love. Ruthlessly despoiled of his love, he vents himself in a rage that buries him in despair, at last to awaken to the only secret of character-formation, viz., that one must lose self not in an isolated love, but in a world-wide passion for righteousness, liberty, and mankind.

Whatever may be said by the peace party, and the Manchester School, as to the vagaries of this poem in its sentiments on war and commerce, one thing is certain—the principle underlying the poem is as eternal as the heavens. Selfish peace is the devil's curse—it makes men cruel, mean and crafty; while, again and again, a just war has given new life to the noble who declared it, and to the brave who waged it.

Tennyson is the poet of moods. Remembering this, much he has written will be read in a clearer light, and with suggestive and delightful results.

# VII.

*BROWNING, THE OPTIMIST.*

## VII.
## BROWNING, THE OPTIMIST.

BROWNING may be spoken of as the apostle of hope. He seldom touches a note of sadness; and when he does, it is only that he may follow and complete it with the note of triumph and faith. His is the poetry that makes men, and having made them, makes them make the best of life. He never wraps our hearts in gloom, nor paralyzes our hands with fear, nor unnerves our footsteps with uncertainty. He is positive, valorous and trustful. His two verities are God and the soul: his key truth concerning the former—that God is love; and concerning the latter—that man is endlessly progressive. To Browning there are no such things as accidents, and no such things as failures. 'God's in His heaven: all's right with the world;' and 'that which God counts blest can't prove accursed.' Nor are these mere assertions on the poet's part, as we shall see. He has fought for his foothold, and holds it not as the sinecure, but as the honest toiler; and, having gained this foothold, he seeks to raise others to his level, and to his range of vision. No charge is more baseless than the common one that Browning is 'an easy-going optimist.' Optimist he is—easy-going he is not. He has dug deep and found rock. Thereon, and therefrom, he builds—not wood, hay, and stubble—but gold, silver, and precious stones.

And now let me try and discover to you the bottom rock which Browning has bared, and upon which he has built. It is this—'God is love.' You say—'Ah, everybody knows that.' The question is, does everybody believe it? Is their knowledge proven in the attitude they preserve amid the dance of circumstance? For they who have firm faith in God's love cannot doubt—cannot be despondent—cannot be craven-hearted! It was this irremovable faith on Browning's part that made him an optimist. And I will tell you how he found it, and show you how he kept it. In the poem entitled 'Christmas Eve' he tells us that in his youth he looked at the silent stars, and saw in them 'power'—'God's visible power.' Yet withal, in his heart, he felt 'that love was the nobler dower.' Do you see that truth? It is self-evident to every thoughtful mind. Love is a grander thing than power—grander every way. If this be so, then behind the visible power of the universe there must be love —for power, without love, would be an incomplete thing— an ungodlike thing, for

> 'A loving worm beneath its clod
> Were diviner than a loveless God
> Amid His worlds.'

Grasp that truth, and you have grasped the key to Browning's position. The stars indicate power—power immense, omnipotent. But if there is nothing beyond them, then the poor, degraded, sin-stained woman who clasps her child of sin to her bosom, the one warm place, is diviner than the God who made the stars, for she loves—and such love is mightier, grander far, than power. Therefore, if we believe in God at all we must believe He is love—love first and last—all love.

Ay! and love with wisdom and power as its instruments. If, then, God be love—with wisdom to direct and power to fulfil—what can go wrong, either in this world or in any other?

Now, it is essential you should grasp that argument. If there be a God He must be a God of love, or He is no God at all; for it is love that makes a God, because love is the crowning attribute of any life, and of all life. If God be not love, where does our love come from? Is it self-made? Love, as the element of moral life, can be no more self-created than can force in physical life. The fact that it is in us, manifesting itself in affection, in sacrifice, and in devotion to others, clearly shows that from some source it proceeded, and that source is God. Granted, however, that it is self-created. Very well. Then we, as loving worms, beneath the clod, are diviner than a loveless God amid His worlds, for we are crowned, though we be below, while He is crownless, though throned above.

Now, all Browning's poetry turns upon this pivot: If God is love, and if He is in His heaven, all is right with the world. If God is love, what He blesses can never be accursed. If my love to my child is only crippled by my inabilities from lack of power, and not from lack of will, what will not God do for me, whose will and power are the servants of His love? And this principle Browning applies to every imaginable phase of life. The men who, like the hero in Pauline, and who, like Paracelsus, cultivate the intellect at the expense of the affection, stumble in darkness and err in unbelief; while a simple, childlike trust in the unfathomable love of a Father leads to the clear and unshaken confidence of a girl like Pippa, and of a man like Lazarus, as portrayed in 'Karshish.'

Out of this great truth Browning educes the correlative truth of immortality. In his own words, there are but two real and abiding things—God and the soul. And I know of no writer who piles argument upon argument so convincingly on behalf of man's immortality as Browning. What means, he asks, the incompleteness of man as measured by the time element—the prophecies which he never lives on earth to fulfil—the ideals which he can never attain to encumbered by the flesh? Is the highest and best voice in us a false voice, or is it true? If God is love, He will neither deceive nor befool. No. And just as our children trust us, and accept our veracity of statement in proportion to their realization of our love, so with men and their Father in heaven.

Now, I think, you will all see how a faith like this begets hope, and how such hope yields strength. No man holding Browning's faith can be a coward. Death and duty will neither terrify nor deter. Nor can any man holding his faith be a pessimist, for faith in an eternal love clears the sky of all clouds, and determines a victorious voyage over the most distant sea. Pessimism not only grows out of Godlessness, but out of a gloomy faith in Omnipotence divorced from love. Where, however, love rules and power serves, you have the root of the glorious optimism that the Teacher of Nazareth foreshadowed when He prayed that His joy might remain in us so that our joy might be full.

One of Browning's key-truths, then, is Love—the soul of the universe. In other words, Love, the foundation of life, the bottom rock upon which God builds; love, the consummation of life, the top-stone of the structure at which the race has sweat and toiled, and told its tale of bricks;

and love, the interpretative key of the vast design of life, which the surveyors and builders view but in parts and pieces, and so view amiss. Grasp that truth, and you hold the fort of Browning's philosophy and poetry.

Take the following poem, entitled 'Wanting is—what?' as beautifully expressive of this truth, and remember that in it Browning supposes himself to be looking out upon a Godless, or loveless, world. In such a world, What is wanting?

> ' Wanting is —— what?
> Summer redundant,
> Blueness abundant,
> — Where is the blot?
> Beamy the world, yet a blank all the same,
> — Framework which waits for a picture to frame.
> What of the leafage, what of the flower?
> Roses embowering with naught they embower!
> Come then, complete incompletion, O comer,
> Pant through the blueness, perfect the summer!
> Breathe but one breath
> Rose-beauty above,
> And all that was death
> Grows life, grows love,
> Grows love!'

Do you want me to mar that gem by throwing it into a vulgar, or, as some would say, a simple, form? I will try. What is the universe without the soul of Love? A universe concerning which it may be said, 'One thing is lacking'—a world, despite its manifold wonders, in which one thing is needful. True, you have the glory of summer-tide—the abundant blueness of the heavens. But what of these? There is a want—a blot. The brightness does not fill up the blank. There is a magnificent frame, but where is the picture if love—if Divine personality—be wanting? There is the foliage of the forest, there is the fragrance and beauty of the flowers; but what do they embower if there be no great Creator whose beauty they show forth? Apart from Him, the soul of Love, all is incompleteness; and before incompleteness can become completeness, a Comer must come, one whose breath is sweeter than the fragrance of the rose, and whose glory outshines the tide of summer; and when He comes a dead universe is instinct with life, and instinct with love.

Another of Browning's great truths is the undying progression of man. He treats death with contempt. What can it do when it has done its worst? Only break the shell, and free the songster—only slough the skin, and let loose the wings—only put off the mortal that mortality may be swallowed up of life! For example, take his poem entitled 'Prospice.'

> 'Fear death?—to feel the fog in my throat,
>   The mist in my face,
> When the snows begin, and the blasts denote
>   I am nearing the place,
> The power of the night, the press of the storm,
>   The post of the foe;
> Where he stands, the Arch Fear in a visible form,
>   Yet the strong man must go:
> For the journey is done and the summit attained,
>   And the barriers fall,
> Though a battle's to fight ere the guerdon be gained,
>   The reward of it all.
> I was ever a fighter, so—one fight more,
>   The best and the last!
> I would hate that death bandaged my eyes, and forebore,
>   And bade me creep past.
> No! let me taste the whole of it, fare like my peers
>   The heroes of old,
> Bear the brunt, in a minute pay glad life's arrears
>   Of pain, darkness and cold.

> For sudden the worst turns the best to the brave,
>   The black minutes at end,
> And the elements' rage, the fiend-voices that rave,
>   Shall dwindle, shall blend,
> Shall change, shall become first a peace out of pain,
>   Then a light, then thy breast,
> O thou soul of my soul! I shall clasp thee again,
>   And with God be the rest.'

I venture to rank that as one of the victorious death-songs of the world, fit to stand side by side with Isaiah's 'Death shall be swallowed up in victory,' and Paul's 'The time of my departure is at hand.' This, indeed, is optimism—nay, it is more, for optimism is but hope, and this is triumph.

And now you ask me, what was the basis of this triumph? Was it mere sentiment? or, worse, was it mere brag? Nay, Browning bases it upon argument—argument irrefragable and clear. You will find, as you read him, that many of his poems are mighty defences built up on its behalf, as, for example, in 'Cleon.'

Just as the poem entitled 'Wanting is—What?' sets before us the incompletion of a universe without God, in like manner this poem entitled 'Cleon' sets before us the incompleteness of man's life when shorn of immortality. It is supposed to be an epistle by a Grecian philosopher and poet, in reply to an inquiry respecting life's problems made to him by an imaginary tyrant called Protus, who, in his admiration of Cleon, and of Cleon's works, longs for the immortal praise and glory that, outliving the philosopher, will yield him a posthumous immortality.

The commencement of the poem introduces us to Cleon, who thanks Protus for the costly gifts accompanying his letter of inquiry, and aspiration after an unknown life; and then goes on to praise Protus for his aspiration, which he likens to the building of a tower, not for building's sake, but that his soul might at last rest atop and view the east. This is a beautiful figure, and in it Browning sets forth the aspiration of the pagan world after the unknown future—ever building—ever climbing—ever looking—led on by the hope of reaching an eventual rest.

Cleon then proceeds to acknowledge the attainments which Protus attributes to him—Yes, it is true he wrote the Epos, composed the little chant, imaged the sun-god, and originated three books upon the soul. In brief, 'All arts are his.' Well, what of these? All the people know it, and recognise it, just as Protus does, with this abatement, that the men of his day, and Cleon with them, though greater than their forerunners, do not look so great to, nor are counted so great by, their contemporaries the crowd. In other words, Cleon's greatness is not recognised by the mass as was the greatness of his early predecessors, and the reason is, that those who judge the present, and the men of the present, judge only by a part of a man, and not by the man in his entirety. Nevertheless, each age is greater than its predecessor, and however great the heroes of old, the heroes of to-day are greater. We have no right to view man apart from men; the soul's achievements are meant to be looked at eventually as a great whole, and not isolated and analysed in parts. Each part has a reference to all, and no part can be pronounced complete without its complemental and succeeding part. The ages do not obliterate one another, but complete one another. When an artist paints a picture, his last colours and shades do not destroy the earlier colours and shades. The first, though hidden, are part of the perfect finish. This, Cleon argues, is progress. Not to argue that the former days are better than these, or that the heroes of old out-gianted the giants of to-day. No! If this were so, there would be no progress. It is only the vulgar who go back, and match man against man in odious comparison. In the evolution of the race there is first the portion of mankind, then the combinations. The heroes of old were great in single acts, their successors are great in multiform acts. A little water in a sphere may be made to touch every part of the sphere if it be rightly manipulated; but the finer air, neither so palpable nor obvious, touches the whole circumference of the sphere when emptied, and fills it more fully than the water did. And yet the vulgar call the sphere full when they see the water, and empty when the water is replaced by air, not knowing air's more hidden properties. Thus men think the world is retrogressing because they miss the so-called greatness of the heroic ages, and fail to see in the composite age, and the composite man, a greater thing than they see in the isolated age and the isolated man.

Now, I want you to grasp this thought of progress. It is a marvellously fine one. Progress is advance from the portion to the combination, from the individual to the race, or, as Herbert Spencer would say, from the simple to the complex. Let me illustrate it. Let us take two men separated by a distance of three thousand years—Plato and Gladstone. Which of the two is the greater man? You say Plato. Cleon—or Browning if you like, for he makes Cleon his mouthpiece—would say Gladstone. And why?

Because in Plato you see a man great in one direction, in Gladstone you see a man great in many directions. Plato might reach farther than Gladstone; but he only touched one point. Gladstone may not have so long a reach, but he has a wider sweep. In the former you have the 'portion,' in the latter you have the 'combination.' A little water in a sphere may be made to touch every point, but only one point at a time, but when the sphere is filled with air, though invisible to vulgar eyes, the whole hemisphere is reached. This is the march of the ages, this is the inheritance of him who is the heir, and not the founder, of the ages. Cry up your heroes of old. Your men of to-day, though less palpably so, are greater and better. Then Cleon proceeds:

> 'I have not chanted verse like Homer, no—
> Nor swept string like Terpander, no—nor carved
> And painted men like Phidias and his friend:
> I am not great as they are, point by point.
> But I have entered into sympathy
> With these four, running these into one soul,
> Who, separate, ignored each other's art.'

The next portion of the letter is given to answering a question submitted by Protus as to whether or not Cleon has not in his great works of genius gained the very crown and end of life. Says Protus, comparing the short-lived fame of a king with the long-lived fame of a philosopher, artist and poet:

> 'Thou leavest much behind, while I leave naught.
> Thy life stays in the poems men shall sing,
> The pictures men shall study; while my life,
> Complete and whole now in its power and joy,
> Dies altogether with my brain and arm,
> Is lost indeed; since, what survives myself?'

Here we have the instinct of the human, after posthumous immortality. Now, note how Cleon meets it, pagan though he be, by throwing out one of those strange feelers after immortality, now and again peculiar to the old pagan world, and in which he shows the utter inadequacy of any kind of immortality save that brought to light, and confirmed, by Christianity. Cleon asks—Why was man made other than a beast? Why was he made self-conscious? Why was he made with capacities for enjoyment he could never fill, and aspirations after truth he could never reach? Better no self-consciousness, no infinity of desire, than that such consciousness and desire should be made to be mocked. Now, here is a root-thought, viz., that self-conscious life must have eternity for its fulfilment. You look at the brute world, and what do you see?

> ' All's perfect else : the shell sucks fast the rock,
> The fish strikes through the sea, the snake both swims
> And slides, forth range the beasts, the birds take flight,
> Till life's mechanics can no further go.'

In other words, in the brute creation, everything achieves its end—the end of its being—' Life's mechanics can no further go.'

> ' And all this joy in natural life is put
> Like fire from off thy (Zeus) finger into each,
> So exquisitely perfect is the same.
> But 'tis pure fire, and they mere matter are ;
> It has them, not they it.'

Browning never put a greater truth in grander form. ' They mere matter are ; life has them, and not they it.' That is, though living, they are not self-conscious. There is mechanism, but not soul. But when man was made he was made self-conscious.

> ' A quality arose within his soul,
> Which, intro-active, made to supervise

> And feel the force it has, may view itself,
> And so be happy.'

Ah! but there's the rub. 'Be happy?' How can he be happy? The beast can, because the beast attains the end of his being, and answers his purpose. But man has desires and powers which, if he be not immortal, must for ever remain unfulfilled, and which, after all, only make a mock of him. The beast, God's lower work, is complete in itself. Man, God's highest work, if not immortal, is incomplete—a total failure, a cruel travesty.

> 'In man there's failure, only since he left
> The lower and inconscious forms of life.'

Take immortality from man, and what does he resemble? In his thirst after enjoyment, in his capacity for endless progression, in his aspirations after the unattainable, he is like

> 'A tower that crowns a country. But alas,
> The soul now climbs it just to perish there!
> For thence we have discovered
> There's a world of capability
> For joy, spread round about us, meant for us,
> Inviting us; and still the soul craves all,
> And still the flesh replies, "Take no jot more
> Than ere thou clomb'st the tower to look abroad!
> Nay, so much less as that fatigue has brought
> Deduction to it."'

And then Cleon goes on to say: The more we desire the more we are mocked. 'Life's inadequate to joy.' The capacity is there. Where the fulfilment, when death ends all?

But he imagines Protus replying, 'Is there not joy in thy works?' Ah! joy is one thing, and *feeling* joy another. Nay, his very works mock him as he toils at them.

> 'Because in my great epos I display
> How divers men, young, strong, fair, wise, can act—

> Is this as though I acted? If I paint,
> Carve the young Phœbus, am I therefore young?'

And then there follows the still keener irony:

> 'Every day my sense of joy
> Grows more acute, my soul more enlarged, more keen;
> While every day my hairs fall more and more,
> My hand shakes, and the heavy years increase—
> The horror quickening still from year to year,
> The consummation coming past escape,
> When I shall know most, and yet least enjoy—
> When all my works wherein I prove my worth,
> Being present still to mock me in men's mouths,
> Alive still, in the praise of such as thou,
> I, I the feeling, thinking, acting man,
> The man who loved his life so over-much,
> Sleep in my urn. It is so horrible,
> I dare at times imagine to my need
> Some future state revealed to us by Zeus,
> Unlimited in capability
> For joy, as this is in desire for joy.'

Wanting is—what? A world without a God of Love is cold, cheerless, and dreary. A soul with unlimited capacity and a limited life is a mockery and a sham.

Thus Browning has painted for us both wants, and pointed us to both fulfilments.

If, then, man is immortal, his outlook of life will not be Cleon's, but rather such an one as Browning gives us in Rabbi Ben Ezra. Let us now turn to the life-philosophy of this grand old teacher, none other than Browning himself. Listen to his opening notes:

> 'Grow old along with me.'

Why, that was the very thing Cleon and Protus dreaded. They anticipated age with terror. With them it was

> 'The horror quickening still from year to year.'

Not so with this grand old optimist, Ben Ezra.   No!

> 'Grow old along with me !
> The best is yet to be,
> The last of life, for which the first was made :
> Our times are in His hand
> Who saith, "A whole I planned,
> Youth shows but half ; trust God ; see all, nor be afraid !"'

You will please observe the words: 'Youth shows but half.' This is the keynote of the poem. Life on earth is divided between youth and age, and the poet proceeds to show how a noble life may be evolved out of both. Let us take first the period of youth. It is either retrogressive—going back to the brute; or progressive—moving onward and upward to the angel. If the former be the course determined upon, then the soul becomes the servant of the flesh :

> 'What is he but a brute
> Whose flesh has soul to suit?'

If the latter be the course decided upon, then flesh helps soul, and each faculty in our animal nature becomes an instrument in the attainment of soul-perfection.

But how is flesh to be subordinated to these higher ends? Listen :

> ' Rejoice we are allied
> To That which doth provide
> And not partake, effect and not receive !
> A spark disturbs our clod ;
> Nearer we hold of God
> Who gives, than of His tribes that take, I must believe.'

In other words Browning says : We stand between two forces—moulding and shaping forces—we are clay—'clods;' but in us there is a spark, ethereal and divine, that disturbs us, then transfixes us. Now this spark is the God-element in us. It allies us to God, and dissociates us from the beast. We are nearer to God than to his tribes, *i.e.*, the fishes, birds, and beasts. We are nearer to Him who provides than to the brutes who receive. Here Browning combats what Carlyle calls the doctrine of dirt, or the material origin of man. Says our poet—We are more than brute, we are divine, for we are allied to the Divine. Clods? Yes! But

> 'A spark disturbs our clod;
> Nearer we hold of God
> Who gives, than of His tribes that take.'

Thus we stand between two forces—the lower and the higher. The clod may sink to brute level, and there be finished and finite; or it may rise even higher and higher towards the God-level, and though never attaining to it, yet always be the nearer for the effort after its attainment. If the former, then although the stomach be full, and the head pillowed on down, and lazy content like a dreamy atmosphere brings with it rest:

> 'Such feasting ended, then
> As sure an end to men.'

Yes, the man has gone; only the brute remains. The noble, the possible God, is eliminated.

But to save us from thus settling on our lees, and thus drifting backward, God has fronted us with elements that rouse soul-powers and call for conflict. He has not let us alone:

> 'Then welcome each rebuff
> That turns earth's smoothness rough,
> Each sting that bids nor sit nor stand but go!
> Be our joy three-parts pain!
> Strive, and hold cheap the strain;
> Learn, nor account the pang; dare, never grudge the throe.'

In other words, if you are thrown upon a bed of thorns rather than upon a bed of roses, thank God for it. The scent of the rose-couch may breathe you off into slumber, but the sting of the thorn may rouse you into the activity of progression.

Thus, every young man stands between a choice—the finite clod—the brute; and the transformed clod—the infolding and developing god. Towards this latter consummation nothing so helps us as the rough rather than the smooth, the sting rather than the stroking down. I would that every young man would take to heart and rejoice in this teaching of Browning's. The young man of to-day is too often content to be the clod without the fire. He eats and drinks and sleeps. If he is one who has to work, he either works because he is compelled, or works that he may amass wealth. His spare moments are moments of gratification; his delirium one of lust and sin. His ideal life is either where there is no factory, or else where there is nothing save money, and all that money brings. Duty is drudgery, time is a task-master, work is weariness, and pleasures only to him are counted profitable. Shame on him! Browning would say.

> 'Poor vaunt of life indeed,
> Were man but formed to feed
> On joy, to solely seek and find and feast:
> Such feasting ended, then
> As sure an end to men:
> Irks care the cropful-bird?
> Frets doubt the maw-crammed beast?'

Rejoice, rather, young men, that true life is conflict and not content; ascending and aspiring, aspiring and ascending, though the top be the unreachable stars. Only thus can you escape the 'finished and finite clod.' But having escaped it,

> 'Thence shall I pass, approved
> A man, for aye removed
> From the developed brute; a god, though in the germ.'

Not a god yet, you observe? but a god in the germ. A clod in the flame, the clay transfixed with fire; ready to face the future because you have proved the past. Listen to the teaching of Browning concerning the next stage in life—the stage of manhood:

> 'And I shall thereupon
> Take rest, ere I be gone
> Once more on my adventure brave and new;
> Youth ended, I shall try
> My gain or loss thereby;
> Leave the fire ashes, what survives is gold;
> And I shall weigh the same,
> Give life its praise or blame;
> Young, all lay in dispute; I shall know, being old.'

In other words, wisdom comes with experience. Age brings knowledge. With youth all was tentative, with age all may be known. The right, the good, the infinite—these we may be as sure of as we are our hands are our own. Then Browning addresses himself to answer the objection that we cannot know truth because no two schools agree as to what truth is, and that therefore as age creeps on all lies in dispute. No, says he, this is not so.

> 'Now, who shall arbitrate?
> Ten men love what I hate,
> Shun what I follow, slight what I receive;
> Ten, who in ears and eyes
> Match me; we all surmise,
> They this thing, and I that: whom shall my soul believe?'

We have all been in that dilemma. Some say this thing, and others that. Which is right, and which are we to follow? The answer lies here—a true man always knows the higher from the lower path: nay, he knows the higher of two high paths. By instinct he can detect, though he may not follow, the highest and best in him, and possible to him. In taking our stand, in making our choice, we must be, as men, true to our highest selves. It is not what others say or what others praise; it is not in majorities nor in popularities. No:

> ' Not on the vulgar mass
> Called " work " must sentence pass,
> Things done, that took the eye and had the price;
> O'er which, from level stand,
> The low world laid its hand,
> Found straightway to its mind, could value in a trice.'

What though the low world vote for loudness and fanfare, for wealth and show, for the moment's sensation and for the moment's possession, are these to seduce the man from right? No; rather

> ' But all, the world's coarse thumb
> And finger failed to plumb,
> So passed in making up the main account;
> All instincts immature,
> All purposes unsure,
> That weighed not as his work,
> Yet swelled the man's amount.'

In other words, there is a great deal of unseen material ever going to make up the character of the true man; a great deal no one knows anything of but God. But although unseen and unknown, it is swelling the man's account. For example, such things as

> ' Thoughts hardly to be packed
> Into a narrow act,
> Fancies that broke through language and escaped;
> All I could never be,
> All men ignore in me,
> This, I was worth to God,
> Whose wheel the pitcher shaped.'

The world measures a man by what he does and by what he is. Browning says God measures a man by what he desires and aspires to be—by thoughts he cannot reduce to acts—by desires he cannot even put into his prayers. By the perfection he strives after, and to which he can never attain—by the failures in attempts at the ideal at which the fools of this world laugh and sneer. But what the vulgar mass sneers at as sin, God looks at as falls in the man's attempt to walk.

Then Browning returns to the clod—the clay. Whatever else may perish two things remain, God and the soul; 'Potter and clay endure.' The clay is on the wheel of plastic circumstance, and the Divine Hand moulds, while time spins the wheel. Here is the soul, the clay, the clod, leavened with the Divine and its possibilities. Here is the world, its surroundings, circumstances, ups and downs, all plastic, not iron-bound, but

> ' Machinery just meant
> To give thy soul its bent,
> Try thee, and turn thee forth, sufficiently impressed.'

Here is time—the years, the earlier ones running swift and joyous, the latter ones bringing the graver mood. But over all there is the Master's hand, and the Master's plan designing and moulding—what? A soul, which Browning likens to a cup. And what is the cup meant for? It is meant for the Master's table; nay, more, it is meant for the Master's lips. Thus man is being moulded here by God's own hand, as time turns the wheel amid the mechanism of circumstance, that at last he may be

> ' Heaven's consummated cup,'

Browning ending with these words ;

> 'So, take and use Thy work:
> Amend what flaws may lurk,
> What strain o' the stuff, what warpings past the aim!
> My times be in Thy hand!
> Perfect the cup as planned!
> Let age approve of youth, and death complete the same.'

This is optimism. Man's dignity and hope lie in the fact that he is for God's use. The rebuffs and stings, the slings and arrows of fortune, are factors in the completion of his life and of his life's service. The man as God means him to be is the spiritual man—the form and life the world's coarse eye cannot see, nor her coarse thumb measure. In the making up of this spiritual man, unuttered thoughts, unattainable desires, are factors of growth and strength. Compare this, I ask you, with the hopelessness of Cleon, and the antithesis, I think, will be explanatory and profitable.

Now, a man with such a life-creed as this will be altogether indifferent to death; he will never be in bondage to its fear. The reality of life will be so real that the negation of death will sink into nothingness. The late Lord Houghton was wont to say that his happiest moments and most delightsome tasks were always blighted with the shadow of death. Browning's faith, as set forth in Rabbi Ben Ezra, treats death with contempt. Let him come and do his worst. The cup is made for the Master, and for the Master's lips.

The full teaching of this truth is illustrated in 'The Grammarian's Funeral,' to which poem I now turn. The old Grammarian was one who could not be diverted from his studies even by death, and like a soldier at his post in the hour of danger, he died grinding at grammar, and Browning idealizes his funeral.

The poem commences by describing a group of the

Grammarian's disciples carrying his corpse towards the place of interment, the hour chosen being that of dawn. One of these disciples, the spokesman, who talks to us through the poem, cries to his comrades:

> 'Let us begin and carry up this corpse,
>   Singing together.
> Leave we the common crofts, the vulgar thorpes
>   Each in its tether
> Sleeping safe on the bosom of the plain,
>   Cared-for till cock-crow:
> Look out if yonder be not day again
>   Rimming the rock-row!'

The place of interment is the mountain-heights; for such a noble soul as this old Grammarian's is worthy of sky-lit summits rather than the gloom of the plain.

> 'Leave we the unlettered plain its herd and crop;
>   Seek we sepulture
> On a tall mountain, citied to the top,
>   Crowded with culture!'

And why morning for his interment, and mountain-heights for his grave?

> 'Our low life was the level's and the night's;
>   He's for the morning.'

Then comes a description of the old Grammarian. He was a man born with the face and throat of Apollo. Long he lived nameless, his youth spent at learning. Then youth passed, and age crept on with its cramped limbs and diminished forces. Well, what did he do? Did he throw down his books, vexed with the world because it had neglected him, soured because the prizes had passed to others, and he was left alone, too old to labour longer? No! Oh no!

> 'He knew the signal, and stepped on with pride
>   Over men's pity;

> Left play for work, and grappled with the world
>     Bent on escaping.'

Thus, in his last moments he donned his professor's gown, and gathered his students around him, asking for the scroll. He was bald, with eyes like lead, and a voice almost silenced with the throttling finger of death. They ask him to desist; they tell him he has mastered the text. This he admits, but replies, 'Still there's the comment.' Other men, seeing the sands of life were thus running out, would have said:

> '"Time to taste life. Up with the curtain."
> This man said rather "Actual life comes next."'

Thus the leader of the funeral procession praises their master's true valour and defiant persistence in work in face of death.

Now the procession reaches the town-gate and the market-place. This rouses the leader of the procession to more panegyric, which he manages to get in between the pauses of the grand funeral hymn. And thus Browning describes the scene (remember the leader of the procession is keeping up the time of the processional hymn, and talking loudly between the pauses):

> '(Here's the town-gate reached; there's the market-place
>     Gaping before us)
> Yea—this in him was the peculiar grace
>     (Hearten our chorus!)
> That before living he'd learn how to live—
>     No end to learning;
> Earn the means first—God surely will contrive
>     Use for our earning.
> Others mistrust and say, "But time escapes;
>     Live now or never!"
> He said, "What's time? Leave 'Now' for dogs and apes:
>     Man has Forever."'

And so crying, the leader describes how the old Grammarian

went back to his books racked with calculus, and how, when his disciples bade him take a little rest, he returned to his studies 'fierce as a dragon.'

Then comes the following marvellous passage, full of fire and titanic force—a kind of commentary on the Grammarian's life, still spoken by the leader:

> 'Oh, if we draw a circle premature,
>     Heedless of far gain,
> Greedy for quick returns of profit, sure
>     Bad is our bargain!
> Was it not great? did not he throw on God
>     (He loves the burthen)—
> God's task to make the heavenly period
>     Perfect the earthen?
> Did not he magnify the mind, show clear
>     Just what it all meant?
> He would not discount life, as fools do here,
>     Paid by instalment.
> He ventured neck or nothing—heaven's success
>     Found, or earth's failure:
> "Wilt thou trust death or not?" He answered, "Yes;
>     Hence with life's pale lure!"
> That low man seeks a little thing to do,
>     Sees it and does it:
> This high man, with a great thing to pursue,
>     Dies ere he knows it.
> That low man goes on adding one to one
>     His hundreds soon hit:
> This high man, aiming at a million,
>     Misses a unit.
> That, has the world here—should he need the next,
>     Let the world mind him!
> This throws himself on God, and unperplexed
>     Seeking shall find Him.'

It was even so with the old Grammarian. Still he toiled at his verbs, despite the death-rattle in his throat.

> 'Gave us the doctrine of the enclitic "De,"
> Dead from the waist down.'

At last the lofty crag platform is reached, where the high-flyers of the feathered race—the swallows and curlews—sweep round and sing, while the multitude slumbered below.

> 'Here—here's his place—where meteors shoot, clouds form,
> Lightnings are loosened,
> Stars come and go! Let joy break with the storm,
> Peace let the dew send!
> Lofty designs must close in like effects:
> Loftily lying,
> Leave him—still loftier than the world suspects,
> Living and dying.'

That is indeed a psalm of life—it is the mighty optimistic song of a life lived in the light of eternity rather than within the limits of time.

Let us now turn to Abt Vogler. Abt Vogler, the musician, seated at his organ, and rapt in the ecstasy of harmony, is throwing off from the notes an improvisation or impromptu melody. As it rises and swells, or as it falls and 'grovells blatant,' towering and falling, sweeping out into infinitude of grandeur, then dying away in dreamy maze, he regrets that he cannot bid this structure of sound rush into sight, and take form before the eye, and tarry there for future admiration. He then goes on to show how this temple of sound is raised by pressing down and importuning the keys; how, now apart, and now combined, they hasten to heighten their master's thought. The bass burying his brow with a blind plunge in the deeps, and there building broad on the roots of things, and thus founding well the palace of harmony which rises into sound, to be followed by the trebles that mount and march like excellent minions, crowd upon crowd, and crest upon crest, and raise rampired walls of gold as transparent as glass, higher and higher, until at last the musician reaches the pinnacled glory—reaches it only to find that not the half has been yet attained. For at the very height of these heart-shattering melodies creation itself seems as though drawn by it to reveal all its wonders. Heaven makes effort to reach earth, just as earth has done its best to reach heaven, Browning throwing out the grand conception that not only are harmonies spiritual ladders by which we climb to heaven, but echoes of heavenly strains by which the spiritual presences also come down to us. As the notes leap forth, the slaves to the musician's touch—his touch being the instrument of his fancy—'earth attained heaven, nor was there any more near and far,' *i.e.*, music killed both time and space. Nor was this all; spiritual presences began to people the glare and glow—the musician soaring on his notes communed with the unseen, the spirits of just men made perfect, the wonderful dead 'who had passed through the body and gone, but were back once more to breathe in an old world worth their new.' What never had been before was now realized, and what had been was as it is to be; and what was matched both. Browning meaning that in the harmonies new creations were found, old creations perfected for the moment in the prophecies of what one day they would become, while that which then was—the common and unattractive—stood forth in all the glory of the Divine. Then we have the musician differentiated from the painter and the poet. Had he painted this creation, there it would have stood; had he written it, it would have lived to be told as a tale. But he could do neither. For music is the finger of God—a flash of the will existent behind all laws He has made. And now the strain falls, the melody ceases, the organ is silent, the player sinks back in tears, and the same music is never to be again. Nay, that cannot be—it cannot be lost—for music such as this is but the uninterrupted communion and harmony between man's soul and God's, for all true aspirations, all soul ascensions, are but earth's notes rising up to heaven, and cannot die in air and perish with the ceasing sound. Oh no:

> ' The high that proved too high, the heroic for earth too hard,
>   The passion that left the ground to lose itself in the sky,
> Are music sent up to God by the lover and the bard;
>   Enough that He heard it once; we shall hear it by-and-by.'

So the musician returns to the common chord as he retires to earth:

> ' Give me the keys. I feel for the common chord again,
>   Sliding by semitones till I sink to the minor,—yes,
> And I blunt it into a ninth, and I stand on alien ground,
>   Surveying awhile the heights I rolled from into the deep;
> Which, hark, I have dared and done, for my resting-place is found,
>   The C Major of this life: so, now I will try to sleep.'

In this poem Browning depicts what music is. He is not the first who has tried: he is one of the few who have succeeded. Three men besides himself have left us never-dying descriptions of harmony—Newman, De Quincey, and Tennyson; and now you shall have the three to compare and muse upon with Browning's. Newman says: 'There are seven notes in the scale: make them fourteen: yet what a slender outfit for so vast an enterprise! Out of what poor elements does some great master in it create his new world! Shall we say that all this exuberant inventiveness is a mere ingenuity or trick of art, like some game or fashion of the day, without reality, without meaning? Is it possible that that inexhaustible evolution and disposition of notes, so rich yet so simple, so intricate yet so regulated, so various yet so majestic, should be mere sound, which is gone and perishes? Can it be that those mysterious stirrings of the heart, and keen emotions, and strange yearnings after we know not what, and awful impressions from we know not where, should be wrought in us by what is unsubstantial, and comes and goes, and begins and ends in itself? It is not so; it cannot be. No; they have escaped from some higher sphere: they are the outpourings of eternal harmony in the medium of created sound; they are echoes from our home; they are the voice of angels, or the magnificat of saints, or the living laws of the Divine governance, or the Divine attributes. Something they are besides themselves which we cannot compass, which we cannot utter—though mortal man, and he, perhaps, not otherwise distinguished above his fellows, has the gift of eliciting them.'

Now for De Quincey's description: 'Let any person of musical sensibility listen to the exquisite music composed by Beethoven, as an opening idea for Bürger's "Lenore," the running idea of which is a triumphal return of a crusading host, decorated with laurels and with palms, within the gates of their native city. A spectacle of young men and women flowing through the mazes of an intricate dance under a full volume of music, taken with all the circumstantial adjuncts of such a scene in rich men's halls— the blaze of lights and jewels, the motion, the sea-like undulation of heads, the interweaving of the figures, the self-revolving both of dance and music, never ending still beginning, and the continual regeneration of order from a system of motions which for ever touch the brink of confusion. Such a scene presents a sort of mask of human life, with its whole equipage of pomps and glories, its luxuries of sounds, its hours of golden youth, and the interminable revolution of ages hurrying after ages, and one generation treading upon the flying footsteps of another; whilst all the while the overruling music attempers the mind to the spectacle, the subject to the object, the beholder to the vision. And although this is known to be but one phase of life—of life culminating and in ascent—yet the darker phase is concealed upon the hidden or averted side of the golden arras, known but not felt; or seen but dimly in the rear, crowding into indistinct proportions. The effect of the music is to place the mind in elective attraction for everything in harmony with its own prevailing key.'

And now take Tennyson's description:

> 'Then methought I heard a mellow sound,
> Gathering up from all the lower ground;
> Narrowing in to where they sat assembled
> Low voluptuous music winding trembled,
> Woven in circles.
>
> \* \* \* \* \* \*
>
> Then the music touched the gates and died;
> Rose again from where it seemed to fail,
> Stormed in orbs of song, a growing gale;
> Till thronging in and on, to where they waited,
> As 'twere a hundred-throated nightingale.
> The strong tempestuous treble throb'd and palpitated;
> Ran into its giddiest whirl of sound,
> Caught the sparkles, and in circles,
> Purple gauzes, golden hazes, liquid mazes
> Flung the torrent rainbow round.'

Now we come to Browning in Abt Vogler:

'And the emulous heaven yearned down, made effort to reach the earth
\* \* \* \* \* \* \*
Novel splendours burst forth, grew familiar and dwelt with mine,
Not a point nor peak but found and fixed its wandering star:
Meteor-moons, balls of blaze: and they did not pale nor pine,
For earth had attained to heaven, there was no more near nor far.
Nay more: for there wanted not who walked in the glare and glow,
Presences plain in the place: or, fresh from the Protoplast,
Furnished for ages to come, when a kindlier wind should blow,
Lured now to begin and live, in a house to their liking at last;
Or else the wonderful Dead who have passed thro' the body and gone,
But were back once more to breathe in an old world worth their new;
What never had been, was now; what was, as it shall be anon;
And what is—shall I say, matched both? for I was made perfect too.'

'Vague writing,' you say. Not vague, but mystical, and bound to be mystical because seeking to throw into words the greatest of all mysteries—music.

And this brings me to say in conclusion that what is termed Browning's vagueness is often mistaken for Browning's mysticism. Heaven has a language as well as earth, and he who seeks to translate it must be content to be despised by the vulgar crowd. Browning soars, and he seeks to tell us on his descent what he has seen. We grovel, and care neither for his heights nor for his message. Paul tells us he saw sights in the third heaven it was not possible for man to communicate. Browning, with Paul's experience, abandons Paul's reserve, and, rushing into song, tells us what he sees. We, poor fools! either sit and stare, or turn aside and mock. We tell him he cannot talk in plain English, that he cannot make simple his message. Did you ever try to write down your highest thoughts and loftiest experiences? If not, sit down and try to do so, and then see how far you succeed; and when you have succeeded, let your friends read your written words, and see how much is plain to them.

There are degrees of poetry—each degree proportionate to its theme. Longfellow sings lowly songs of lowly themes, and his poetry is read by all. Milton sat alone, blind to earth, but with open eye to heaven's splendours, and his words are read by few. We call one simple, the other vague. We should be nearer the mark if we called one simple and the other profound. And it is even so with Browning. To use his own term, he walks 'the rampired heights'—he dwells amid 'the pinnacled glory.' It is not by mastering the rules of grammar and the laws of the English language we train ourselves to understand him, but by going down into the deeps of our own experience, and climbing to the heights of God. And yet from out of the mazes of his music, and the labyrinthine windings of his poetry, the feeblest mind may gather strength and inspiration. God is, and man is; two immortals, yea, rather an infinite and an immortal—God and the soul. Whatever else perishes, these remain. God stoops to man; man rises to God. Thus with a God who is all love, and whose power and wisdom are in servitude to this love, no mistake can be made, no accident can happen; while with a soul vigorous with the seed of eternal life there must ever be the upward look, the onward movement, and the crown and consummation of life. In Browning's words:

> 'There shall never be one lost good! What was shall live as before:
>   The evil is null—is naught—is silence implying sound;
> What was good shall be good, with, for evil, so much good more;
>   On the earth the broken arcs; in the heaven, a perfect round.'

## THE END

www.ingramcontent.com/pod-product-compliance
Lightning Source LLC
Chambersburg PA
CBHW020239170426
43202CB00008B/146